ROLLS-ROYCE HERITAGE TRUST

A VIEW OF ANSTY

1935-1982

David E Williams

HISTORICAL SERIES No 25

Published in 1998 by the
Rolls-Royce Heritage Trust
P O Box 31 Derby England DE24 8BJ

© 1998 D E WILLIAMS

This book, or any parts thereof, must not be reproduced in any form without the written permission of the publisher.

ISBN: 1 872922 12 0

The Historical Series is published as a joint initiative by the Rolls-Royce Heritage Trust and The Sir Henry Royce Memorial Foundation.

Previous volumes published in the series are listed at the rear, together with volumes available in the Rolls-Royce Heritage Trust Technical Series.

Cover Picture: An aerial view of the Ansty site, mid 70s

Books are available from:
Rolls-Royce Heritage Trust, Rolls-Royce plc, Moor Lane, PO Box 31, Derby DE24 8BJ

Origination and Reproduction by Neartone Ltd, Arnold, Nottingham
Printed by Premier Print, Glaisdale Parkway, Bilborough, Nottingham

CONTENTS

Page

Foreword		4
Acknowledgements		5
Introduction		6
Chapter One	Origins	8
Chapter Two	Flying training	10
Chapter Three	The Flying Standards	16
Chapter Four	Other events on the aerodrome	18
Chapter Five	Turbojets and turboprops	19
Chapter Six	The aero engines that came to Ansty	21
Chapter Seven	The move from Parkside to Ansty	27
Chapter Eight	The ten thousand horsepower rig	31
Chapter Nine	P176, a supersonic turbojet	34
Chapter Ten	P181 and 182, the last of the line	39
Chapter Eleven	The high speed diesel	42
Chapter Twelve	Other diversifications	48
Chapter Thirteen	Rockets	60
Chapter Fourteen	Underwater weapons - the unseen activity	72
Chapter Fifteen	A merger and a takeover	75
Chapter Sixteen	4th February 1971, the unthinkable actually happened	80
Chapter Seventeen	Survival and success	85
Chapter Eighteen	Marine gas turbines	86
Chapter Nineteen	Hovercraft, a hope unfulfilled	97
Chapter Twenty	Industrial gas turbines	100
Chapter Twenty-One	Gas and oil	109
Chapter Twenty-Two	New ideas of management	113
Chapter Twenty-Three	People	119
Epilogue		129

FOREWORD

It is a privilege and an honour to have been asked by David to write the foreword for his definitive history of the Ansty site. Anyone who takes the time to read this extremely informative, insightful and, not surprisingly for David, occasionally funny 'histoire' cannot fail to be caught up in the excitement of Ansty nor fail to be captivated by the supreme technical capability and innovation of the Ansty team. Always the 'orphan', indeed more accurately, the "Maverick", they never failed to rise to the occasion of producing a technically challenging solution to a problem that, more often than not, had yet to be identified by their potential customers!

Finally settling on Industrial and Marine Gas Turbines, the team at Ansty did in the end find a market that welcomed their technical innovation and prowess and built an international business that generated adequate returns for its shareholders. I was privileged to be a junior member of that team, working with many of the people identified in this volume. The thing that remains with me today is the enormous freedom of action open to men and women of initiative.

David captures that entrepreneurial spirit in his writing and I wholeheartedly recommend this book to all who want to know about more than aero engines and cars as they seek to understand the "Rolls-Royce heritage".

Colin H Green
Director – Operations, Rolls-Royce plc
Vice President, Rolls-Royce Heritage Trust

ACKNOWLEDGEMENTS

Special thanks are due to Arthur Broomfield for his contributions on 'Rockets', to Nigel Ferriman for his contribution on 'Underwater weapons' and to Brian Slatter for his careful reading and constructive criticism of the text.

A considerable debt is owed to Alva King for her sterling work with the word processor and to John Ellam for the artwork.

INTRODUCTION

Those most closely connected with important events are usually too busy to record the story for posterity. The recapture of history thus involves gathering together episodes, only some of which were adequately recorded at the time. For example, the biographer of Richard Trevethick, writing some six decades later of this great contributor to the Industrial Revolution, wrote that "Practical men are too apt to leave the facts unrecorded".

And so it is with those involved in Britain's aero engine industry. This again was demonstrated when Henry Royce's early achievements in the first decade of the 20th century were being celebrated in Rolls-Royce's 75th Anniversary. At the opening ceremony at Paulerspury were Dennis Head and Roy Heathcote, who expressed concern at the paucity of early records. This was a factor in the foundation of the Rolls-Royce Heritage Trust, the objectives of which include the recording of Company history.

"A View of Ansty" has been written in that context as a record of activities on a Company site in Coombe Fields and Walsgrave-on-Sowe near the village of Ansty in Warwickshire. The business started with the acquisition of land from several adjacent farms to provide an airfield to start a flying school in 1935 and the story continues to the end of 1982 when the Coventry Branch of the Heritage Trust focused its attention on Ansty.

Like the story of the Renaissance, it is not complete of itself but involves threads drawn from other times and other places. To make a better narrative such connected origins have been described. History is full of ifs and buts but the temptation to make value judgements about the decision-making processes has been largely resisted. In any case, "A View of Ansty" is the way the author saw it.

The 20th century history of the Ansty site is typical of the saga of the aero engine industry in a time of rapid and turbulent change. Since the arrival of the Avro training aircraft at the aerodrome at the end of 1935, developments have been spectacular. Typifying the technical advance, the speed of air supported aircraft increased during that time by two orders of magnitude. The Avro trainers of 1935 were simple, small and slow and were little more than a rudimentary framework with wings and a lightweight piston engine.

Before the end of the 1970s the technology of aircraft propulsion systems had advanced in terms of durability, efficiency and cost to the extent that derivatives of this prime mover had successfully invaded the traditional industrial markets of the piston engine and the steam turbine. It is in the adaptation of the aero gas turbine that Ansty became a significant industrial enterprise in its own right and most of this story is involved therein.

The constant background of the aero engine business was one of challenge. Merger, take-over and even collapse of the Company, are all part of the story. The changes and chances of the time led to the demise of many enterprises in the United Kingdom; Ansty shared these tribulations and survived.

A VIEW OF ANSTY

CHAPTER ONE

Origins

The history of the Ansty site in the 20th century stems from the involvement of John Siddeley in aviation. Appointed in 1909 as the General Manager of the Deasy Motor Car Manufacturing Company at Parkside in Coventry, he was to create an enterprise of major size and importance. From this start in 1909, until he retired in 1936 as Sir John Siddeley, "JDS" was to dominate the Armstrong Siddeley organisation and all its subsidiaries. Not a pioneer in the engineering sense, he had however, a legendary genius in applying the skills of the entrepreneur to the technology of his day. Though criticised for a parsimonious attitude to expenditure on development, which arguably caused him to lose the race for the larger radial aero engines, he nevertheless handed on to his successors a thriving industrial empire.

Lord Kenilworth, formerly Sir John Siddeley and the 6 horsepower "Little Siddeley"

During the First World War, JDS had established close business links with Armstrong Whitworth in Newcastle. As the war drew to an end, the two companies recognised the need to adjust to the vastly different trading conditions of peacetime and during the Autumn of 1918 he approached Armstrong Whitworth with a proposal for a joint venture. Thus, in 1919, the Armstrong Whitworth Development Company was formed and aircraft production at Newcastle ceased altogether. The new organisation had a subsidiary by the name of Armstrong Siddeley Motors, the successor to the Siddeley Deasy Motor Company. Both aero engine and aircraft production were centred on Parkside but in 1920 the Company bought an airfield vacated by the RAF at Whitley to which aircraft manufacture was transferred, leaving aero engines, cars and aircraft design at Parkside.

The aviation work of Armstrong Whitworth led to an expansion of activity at Whitley, some of which was later transferred to Baginton. In 1936, the merger of the Hawker and Siddeley interests led to the formation of the Hawker-Siddeley Group and to the retirement of JDS.

CHAPTER TWO

Flying Training

In 1919 and within a year of its formation, the RAF made an explicit commitment so to structure its organisation that it could rapidly expand to meet any likely threat. Appreciating this situation, and aware of the importance of air power, JDS started a Flying School on the outskirts of Coventry, at Whitley. By 1923 a contract had been negotiated to train pilots of the RAF Reserve. Whitley was one of five flying training schools set up at that time in the UK by aircraft manufacturers. In 1930 the RAF Reserve School at Whitley was transferred to a former A V Roe Works at Hamble, later to become Air Service Training Limited, the "University of the Air".

In the years before 1935 the Air Force itself had only a bare minimum of Training Schools. The comfortable axiom within the defence institutions that "Britain was not likely to be involved in a major war within 10 years" meant that there was no set date by which squadrons were to be fully prepared for war. Even the assumption by Hitler of the Chancellorship of Germany in 1933 produced no change in the annual estimates for defence, either in 1933 or 1934. At this time the RAF was pursuing a policy of training within squadrons as an economy measure but the price of economy was unreadiness. In 1934, however, the Defence Requirements Committee called for a five year expansion plan with the object of providing 40 additional squadrons in the near term.

In the Autumn of 1935, the year in which the Messerschmitt Bf109 started its flight development programme, the Minute Book of the Rugby Rural District Council contains an item for 16 September, which reads:

Plans for Aerodrome:

The Surveyor reported that since the date of the last meeting of the Public Health Committee, he had received plans for an aerodrome to be laid out in the Parish of Coombe Fields together with administrative buildings, etc. and he asked the Council to consider same as a matter of urgency. Resolved that the plans now considered to be approved, subject to the approval of the Honorary Town Planning Surveyor.

The minutes of the next meeting in November that year record rather cryptically "Air Raid Precautions – consider precautionary measures against hostile air attack". The clouds of war were coming closer.

In September 1935, Air Service Training, a satellite within the Armstrong Siddeley Development Company, previously the Armstrong Whitworth

Tinted area = 294.734 acres
(or thereabouts)

Scale : five inches to one statute mile

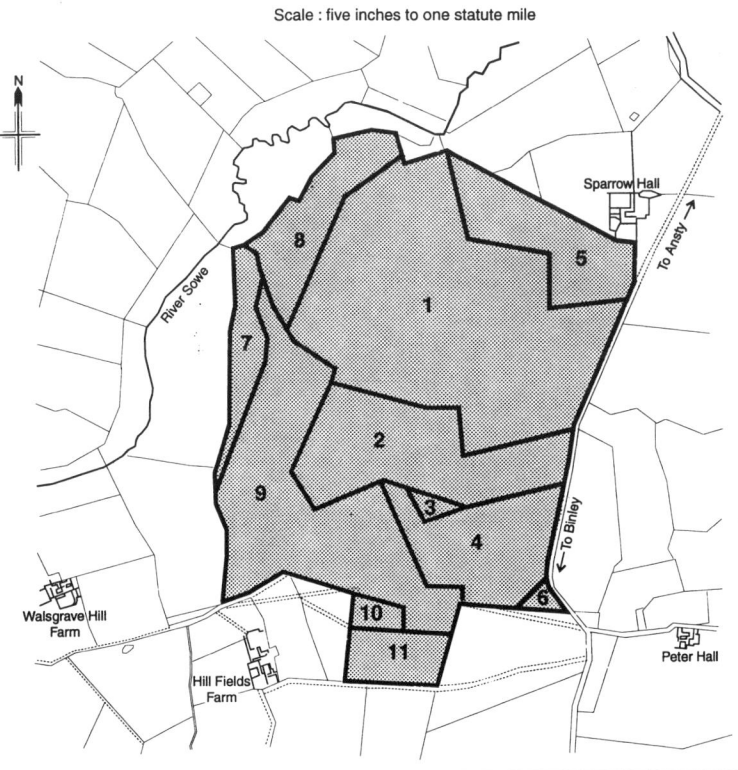

Area	Acres	Date acquired by Air Service Training Ltd.	Purchase price
1	101.276	30th September 1935	£4,557
2	39.165	30th September 1935	£1,418
3	1.540	21st June 1938	£150
4	23.750	14th December 1938	£1,425
5	26.142	21st January 1939	£1,530
6	2.000	13th June 1940	£220
7	12.095	17th December 1948	£605
8	19.671	12th September 1949	£1,180 5. 0d
9	56.357	19th September 1949	£3,000
10	1.988	7th February 1950	£610
11	10.750	26th September 1952	£2000
Total 294.734 acres			**Total £16,695 5. 0d**

Dates of acquisition of Ansty Aerodrome by Air Service Training Limited and purchase prices

Development Company, acquired its first piece of land on the site with the purchase of 101 acres of open land from George Watson who farmed Sparrow Hall Farm, Coombe Fields. In 1982 his son, by then farming in Essex, recalled the arrival of three Armstrong Siddeley cars and a man named Pope who sought to buy about 100 acres of land from his father. The deal went through and another part of the Siddeley empire had been established. This land, shown on the map as Item 1, was supplemented by the purchase at the same time of a further 39 acres from John Vernon of Hill Fields Farm. By September 1952 a total of 11 pieces of land had been acquired (Table I) totalling 294.7 acres. The total purchase price over these years amounted to £16,695.5.0d. Final purchase brought the total area owned by 1982 to 311 acres. Erection of buildings started immediately in September 1935 with the construction near North Gate of a new Hangar, living quarters and the Administration Block. An aerial view of these, together with 15 Avro Trainers on the airfield was probably taken in March or April of 1936; 50 years later all these buildings were still in use.

On the 1st of January 1936, the airfield was officially opened for the basic training of Direct Entry (Short Service Commission and NCO) pilots for the RAF and as an ab initio private flying school also under the aegis of Air Service Training. The aircraft were civilian registered Avro Cadets with Armstrong Siddeley Genet radial engines. On the 6th of January Number 9 ERFTS (Elementary and Reserve FTS) was formed.

View from the North gate in 1935

View from the air in 1936

All flying instructors were ex-RAF personnel with Central Flying School categories. The RAF took over the airfield on 1 January 1940 with Wing Commander RPP Pope as its first CO. The School remained at Ansty until the Ministry of Aircraft Production took the airfield over on 31 March 1944.

In September 1938 Number 4 CANS (Civil Air Navigation School) was formed and attached to Number 9 ERFTS to train navigators both Direct Entry and ERFTS. It was civilian operated until the RAF arrived. SARO Clouds and Mark 1 Avro Ansons were the first navigational trainers. By now Tiger Moths, Magisters, Hawker Harts and Hinds and a Hawker Audax were in service. Frank Broome, a designer at Ansty in the 80s first flew solo in those days in a Tiger Moth. The Volunteer Reserve flew at weekends and the airfield was thus operational for seven days a week. The aerodrome was still remembered in 1982 as an exceedingly busy place. Fred Lockwood, an aeronautical engineer employed at the school, vividly remembered episodes from those days. He recalled the story of G-ATTK, one of the early Avro Cadets taken out by a pupil who had just flown solo. One day, whilst doing circuits and bumps, he flew without permission to demonstrate his newly won skill to his girlfriend in South Wales. On the way back he force-landed near Banbury for fuel and persuaded an AA patrolman to fetch him five gallons. He was missing all day and finally landed by the light of flares. Confronted by an angry CO, the story goes that the hapless pilot said "It's

Frank Broome's first solo

full of Zip, Sir, shall I drain it?". Next morning, after a brief interview with the CO, he was off the premises for good.

Fred Lockwood remembered too, the SARO Clouds, which he recalled were not a suitable aircraft for training. They were powered by two Siddeley Servals mounted on tripods above the wing. They frequently suffered fuel starvation problems and of the original six which joined the School, five were involved in forced landings for this reason. The Cloud was a somewhat clumsy amphibian and a forced landing meant partial dismantling to cart the aircraft away. Only one of them remained at Ansty and the decision was taken to fly it to AST at Hamble. Fred remembered that the pilots drew lots to do this job, Flt Lt Coombes drawing the shortest straw. He took the Cloud back to Hamble with Fred on board.

Alf Gaston, who was general factotum to the CO in the early days, remembered the trainees as "Civilised tearaways but very pleasant chaps". He recalled a high spirited jape by these tearaways who, one weekend whilst the CO was on leave, locked a goat in his office. In addition to the general mayhem discovered on the Monday morning, the goat had eaten the CO's uniform trousers.

Such high-spirited adventures were commonplace and in talking to people in the neighbourhood who were involved in those days, it became clear that Ansty Aerodrome was a place full of interest and excitement for the rural community. In 1939, Ansty Aerodrome was selected as the venue on 20 May for the Empire Air Day. Attended by over four thousand people, it was an event of outstanding interest and as the Press wrote, "The Avro bomber (later to become the Anson)… attracted considerable attention…"

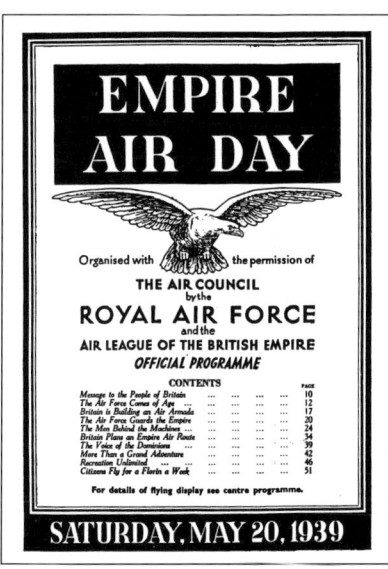

Empire Air Day - 1939

Programme of Events

Event No.	Time	Event
1	14.45 – 15.00	Formation Flying. (Hawker Harts).
2	15.00 – 15.10	Cutting the Ribbon. (Avro Cadet).
3	15.10 – 15.15	Blind Flying Take-off. (Avro Cadet).
4	15.15 – 15.30	Fighter Attack on Ground Target. (3 Hawker Hurricanes).
5	15.30 – 15.45	Individual Acrobatics. (Avro Cadet).
6	15.45 – 16.00	Shallow Dive Bombing Demonstration. (3 Bristol Blenheims).
7	16.00 – 16.15	Pupil and Instructor. (2 Avro Cadets).
8	16.15 – 16.30	Acrobatics and Formation Flying. (3 Avro Cadets).
9	16.30 – 16.45	Synchronized Acrobatics. (2 Hawker Harts).
10	16.45 – 17.05	Air Race. (Avro Anson, Avro Cadet, De Havilland Tiger Moth, Hawker Hart and Hawker Hind).
11	17.05 – 17.15	Landing with Stopped Engine. (Avro Cadet).
12	17.15 – 17.30	Dive Bombing and Low Level Bombing Attack. (6 Fairey Battles).
13	17.30 – 17.45	Air Attack by 3 Hawker Harts on an Avro Anson.
14	17.45 – 18.00	Converging Bombing Attack. (3 Hawker Harts)
15	18.00 – 18.30	Fly Past of Types. (Bristol Blenheim, Harvard, Fairey Battle, Avro Anson, Hawker Hind, Hawker Audax, Armstrong Whitworth Whitley, Hawker Hart, Avro Cadet, and De Havilland Tiger Moth).

After the closure of the now redesignated Number 9 EFTS (Reservists having been dropped at the end of March 1944, no further flying training was undertaken until 1951 when AST, in conjunction with the RAF, trained National Service Pilots, de Havilland Chipmunk trainers being the new workhorses. In March 1953 the post war school Number 2 Basic Flying Training School, like all other civilian operated establishments, was closed as a Government economy measure. The airfield was derequisitioned and returned to the ownership of Air Service Training Limited. The Manager and Chief Instructor, Bert Tribe, who had flown no less than 70 different types of aircraft during his 30 years in the RAF, retired from flying when Number 2 EFTS closed. He then joined Armstrong Siddeley as Engineer-in-Charge of experimental flying at Bitteswell and later became Manager of the Sapphire aero engine repair shop at Ansty.

CHAPTER THREE

The Flying Standards

By the mid 1930s the threat from Nazi Germany had become clear and the Prime Minister, Stanley Baldwin, had announced in the Commons that Britain would aim to achieve parity in the air with Germany. In February 1936 the Cabinet had approved Scheme F, whereby the RAF would be expanded to a total of eight thousand front line aeroplanes, including re-equipment with new aircraft just emerging from the design stage. To achieve this objective the RAF had recognised an urgent need of new sources of production. In May 1936 a meeting was held with car makers in the Midlands, including Captain Black of the Standard Motor Company. The Secretary of State for Air took the Chair and announced what was to become the Shadow Factory Scheme whereby the Austin, Daimler, Rootes, Rover and Standard companies were invited to go separately into the aero engine business. Standards had built RE8 and Sopwith Pup aircraft at Canley during the First War and within three months of the outbreak of hostilities in the

The 500th Mosquito

The last Mosquito

Second War in September 1939 were invited, in addition to their new aero engine commitments, to build 300 Airspeed Oxford Training aircraft at Canley.

To be able to meet this programme the Standard Motor Company, in association with the Ministry of Aircraft Production, built a new assembly and flight test facility at Ansty, by then the home of Number 9 ERFTS. Sub-assemblies were built at Canley and transported to the airfield where they were assembled, flight tested and flown off to the RAF. In 1942 the Oxfords were followed by the assembly, test and delivery of Mosquito FBVI fighter bombers, the first emerging in June 1943. By this time Oxford production was winding down and the last of a total of 750 left the Ansty factory in July 1943.

The first 500 Mosquitos had been built and delivered by the end of 1944. Standards went on to complete a grand total of 1,066. Captain Black, Managing Director of the firm, appears on the left in the picture with the Chief Test Pilot, Sam Williams.

CHAPTER FOUR

Other events on the aerodrome

Noel Roper remembered a curious event in June 1940 when five small enemy bombs fell around Ansty, two of them on the airfield. This was a night attack and it was assumed that the bombs were jettisoned by an aircraft unable to find its intended target. Noel remembered too the building of the runways for the aircraft built by Standards and that rubble from the Coventry Blitz was used in the construction of the perimeter track.

In the years soon after the end of the Second War the runway and perimeter track were used for motor cycle racing, two very successful meetings being held by the Antelope MCC in 1950. The course was one and three quarter miles long, the lap record at the beginning of the season being held by George Brown (998 Vincent HRD) at 84.2 mph. Twelve events were held in April 1950 involving 215 competitors. At the second meeting in October of that year, 253 competitors took part in some 15 events. This was a field day for the Nortons which won each of the last 12 events with Geoff Duke (500 Norton) establishing a new lap record at 87.7 mph. Duke had broken the lap record twice at this meeting on a machine half the size of the Vincent HRD.

The following year saw the resumption of flying training at AST and sadly, therefore, for the motor cycling community, the end of competitions at Ansty.

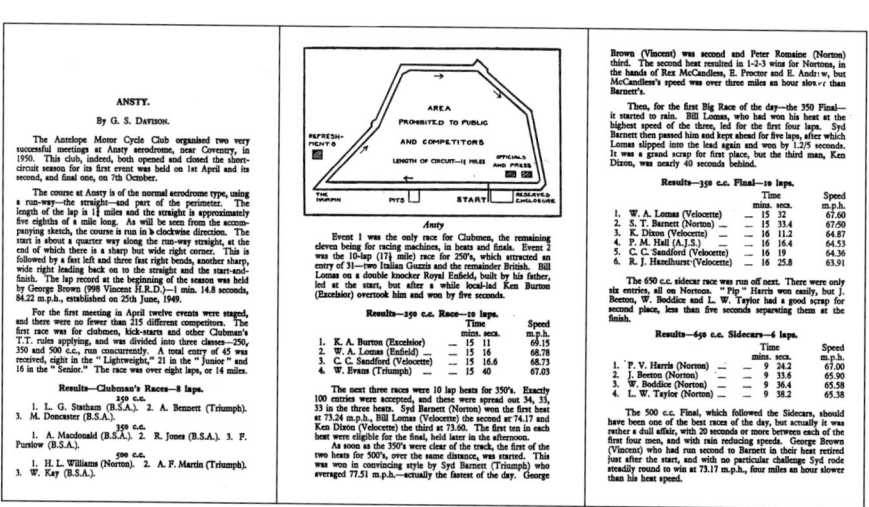

Motorcycling on the aerodrome

CHAPTER FIVE

Turbojets and turboprops

In the period between the two World Wars there were in the UK two mainstreams of development of the aero gas turbine, the Whittle design with its twin entry centrifugal compressor and the RAE design with axial compressors. The Armstrong Siddeley line of gas turbines had its origins in the designs of the Royal Aircraft Establishment (RAE).

One of the most important steps in the evolution of the gas turbine and one of the earliest was taken by A A Griffith, who in 1926 at the RAE, produced an aerodynamic theory of blade design based on the flow past aerofoils as

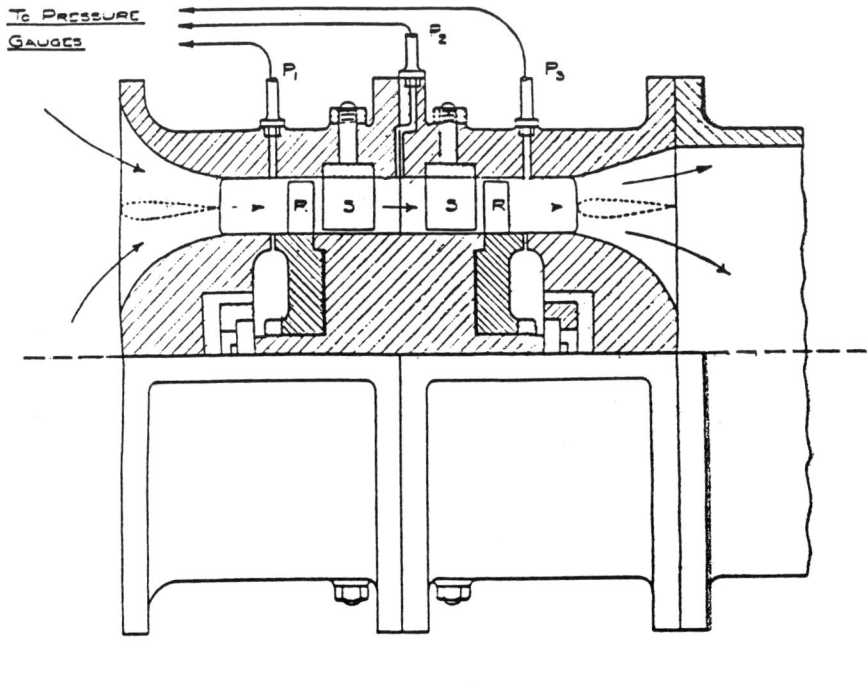

Dr Griffiths' 1926 experiment

distinct from the flow through passages. He was authorised by the Air Ministry and the Aeronautical Research Council to proceed with practical tests. Firstly, these were carried out on cascades of stationary blades in small wind tunnels, a technique widely adopted later in the development of turbomachinery. Secondly, experiments were conducted on a small turbocompressor pair. Even though the blades were only half an inch tall, a high efficiency was obtained which indicated the feasibility of an aero engine based on an axial turbocompressor.

In 1929, Griffith proposed a turbopropeller engine using contra-rotating wheels, each carrying an annulus of turbine blades and an annulus of compressor blades. Although the authorities recommended rig tests, nothing was done until 1939, when Armstrong Siddeley was contracted to build a small version of the Griffith turbocompressor to the design of the RAE. It was a very ambitious design but unfortunately had an indifferent performance. This, together with rapid developments which were taking place with more conventional designs, led to its abandonment by RAE and except for a brief return by Rolls-Royce to the idea, no further development of this configuration occurred. The rapid evolution of axial compressors at the RAE which had started in 1936 was to lead to a total commitment of Armstrong Siddeley to the aero gas turbine.

CHAPTER SIX

The aero engines that came to Ansty

Between 1932, when Frank Whittle had tried unsuccessfully to persuade Armstrong Siddeley Motors to become involved in the gas turbine and June 1942, when ASM began work on the ASX turbojet, the only significant turbine work which had been done at Coventry was the manufacture of the Griffith contra-rotating machine. In 1942, the Company became responsible for the mechanical design and manufacture of the ASX in collaboration with the RAE. The latter had provided the aero and thermodynamic design of the major components and had designed the general layout of the engine. The ASX was an axial jet of 5:1 pressure ratio which took it, in terms of performance, ahead of the contemporary Whittle design. The configuration was novel in that the compressor was turned back to front so that the combustion chambers could be arranged round the outside of the compressor casing. By this means ample length was available for combustion without excessive overall length of engine. The ASX had a design thrust of 2,500 pounds at sea level for a weight of only 1,900 pounds. It first ran in April 1943 and was installed for flight test in a Lancaster in June 1945. The ASX became the first turbine engine to run at Ansty when in 1946 starting trials were carried out in a temporary building on the site of what would later become Number 48 Test House. Meanwhile, a need emerged for a turbine engine for a naval fighter able to take off from a carrier. A project was therefore put in hand to develop the ASX as a turboprop which eventually became the Python. This involved the design of an 8:1 reduction gear running at an input speed of 8000 rpm requiring considerable extrapolation of aero engine practice. The engine first ran in March 1945 and first took to the air in a Lancaster in October 1948.

An important innovation in the ASX/Python was the replacement of the originally intended Lucas combustion chamber by the Siddeley vaporiser design in which fuel and air were mixed and heated in an internal preheater. This was the precursor of a series of vaporiser combustion chambers which would still be applied to new Rolls-Royce engine designs in the 1980s.

All the early testing of the Python was done at Parkside on dynamometer beds. When testing became necessary with its contra-rotating propellers a wing test bed was built at Ansty.

In 1945, the Company was in the early stages of development of an 850 hp radial piston engine and was asked by the Ministry to consider a turboprop instead. The project design of this engine, code name ASZ, which was to become the Mamba, was completed in the Autumn of 1945 and appeared

The Python wing at Ansty

very attractive. With an overall diameter of 27 inches, as compared with 50 inches for the piston engine, the estimated weight was only 650 pounds, as compared with 980 pounds. Running began at Parkside in 1946. Since the fuel consumption of a turbine engine is relatively poor in specific terms at lower power and good at high power, it was later decided for a long range maritime aircraft, to develop the Double Mamba to give twin engine power for take-off and single engine cruising. Each engine drove an independent co-axial propeller. When an engine was required for the Jindivik pilotless target aircraft, a jet derivative of the Mamba was produced. By removing the reduction gear and propeller drive and with minor modifications to the turbine, a thrust of about 1,000 pounds was obtained. This engine, the Adder, first ran in December 1948 and flew in an early piloted version of the aircraft called the Pika. Meanwhile, a purpose-designed short life engine, the Viper, was introduced for the propulsion of target aircraft.

The Viper's design thrust of 1,575 pounds and a ten hour test were achieved in 1951. Simplicity of design was an essential feature of the original Viper and although it was later developed into a highly successful conventional engine, the basic simplicity was retained. The remarkable saga of this small axial turbojet beginning as an expendable engine culminated in a long life engine of outstanding durability still surviving in the market place four decades later.

In the two decades following the first flight of a British jet, the thrust of the most powerful engines had increased 20 fold. The race for higher power was on. The Sapphire was very much a contender. Like the ASX, it was a derivative of the pioneer work of the RAE team which had been led by Hayne Constant. Their endeavours had started in 1936 and by 1939 had produced the design of the F1 axial turbojet. The F1 went to the Metropolitan Vickers Electrical Company where a highly successful programme led, via the F2/4 Beryl, to the F9 Sapphire. By this time Metropolitan Vickers had withdrawn from the aero engine business and eventually the Sapphire came to Coventry. The transfer of responsibility took place in 1947, the Ministry designation MV Sa1 changing to AS Sa1. Bench testing started at Ansty in October 1948. By that time drawings had been issued for a cleaned-up and revised Sa2, which was demonstrated in December 1949 at a thrust of 7,380 pounds as compared to the 6,500 of Sa1. A pair of Sa2s was installed in Lancastrian VM733 and flown in January 1950. The following August two Sa2s were flown in a Meteor and reached an altitude of 39,370 feet in 3 minutes 9 seconds, thereby establishing a World Record.

The Sapphire Meteor

The design office at Parkside had, by now, made the first major changes by the adoption of a Siddeley annular vaporising chamber and the addition of a centre bearing to the rotor. Thus the rotor was changed from a welded-up construction to a combined disc and drum arrangement. This was the Sa3 which passed its acceptance test in April 1950. Bench tests at Ansty during 1951 confirmed that, with relatively minor aerodynamic changes and a small increase in rotor speed, a thrust of 8,300 pounds could be attained. This was the Sa6 which, with an increase in firing temperature, became the Sa12 with a thrust of 8500 pounds. The Sa6/Sa12 went into production in 1953 as the 100 Series. A derivation of the Sa6, with an increased diameter intake, originated in 1951 as the Sa4. By July 1952 Sa4 was delivering a thrust of 9,700 pounds. A fairly extensive redesign, using the lessons of Sa3 to Sa6, was made to Sa4 to become the Sa7 which first ran in August 1952. In the summer of 1953 flight trials were made in a Canberra and a Type Test in October of that year confirmed a thrust of 10,200 pounds at a specific fuel consumption of 0.885 pounds per hour per pound of thrust. In the spring of 1955 Sa7 was type tested at 10,500 pounds.

Further development led to the Sa8 with air cooled turbine blades and to the Sa9 which added a zero (ie additional) stage to the compressor of Sa7. Finally, a project study was completed on the Sa10 which was to combine the cooled blades of the Sa8 with the larger compressor of Sa9. Though Sa8 and Sa9 were run, Sa10 did not advance beyond the project stage. Sa7 went into production as the 200 Series.

Reheat systems were developed for both Sa6 and Sa7. The prototype English Electric P1A (later to become the Lightning) had two Reheat Sa5s with fixed propelling nozzles. Variable boost was required and an unusually wide range of stable burning was therefore necessary. For Sa7 in the Gloster Javelin, increased thrust was needed only at high altitude. It was recognised that the normal fuel pump would have spare capacity at altitude and would suffice to provide both engine and reheat fuel. A reheat system was devised to operate at exceptionally high duct velocity to meet the requirement without increase in jet pipe diameter.

By the end of the 1950s when Sa7 had reached 12,300 pounds of thrust with reheat (designated Sa7R), the end of the road was in sight. Although Sa10 would have been in the 15,000 pound class, Bristol Olympus and Rolls-Royce Conway had arrived with potential to outstrip the Sapphire. The two new contenders would provide for all the needs of the largest civil and military aircraft which could be foreseen. The Sapphire had had its day but its development had been an outstanding achievement. In less than a decade from its arrival in Coventry, very much as a prototype, thrust had been doubled. It had been a pacemaker in powering the first British aircraft to achieve supersonic speed in level flight (P1A) and it had powered the world's

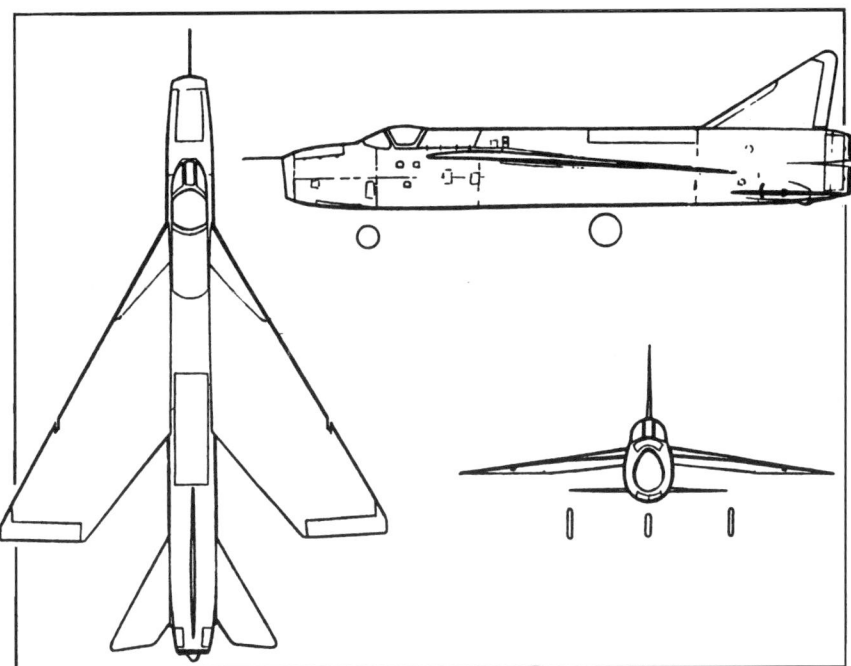

English Electric P1A

first operational delta aircraft (Javelin). Over 11,000 had been built under licence in the United States as the J65 and this engine was still in military service in the Falklands campaign as the engine of the Douglas Skyhawk.

CHAPTER SEVEN

The move from Parkside to Ansty

The continuation of international tension after the Second World War resulted in an ongoing demand for aero engines of increasing performance. There was no shortage of government funds for the development of gas turbines although volume production of existing engines was almost halted. In this situation it was clear that there was considerable potential for the development of new military engines. Armstrong Siddeley, already short of space for test beds at Parkside and constrained by the environmental limitations of an urban site, began in the early 1940s to transfer its aero engine development to Ansty. The development team moved out later to continue its work under the technical leadership of W H Lindsey.

The first gas turbine test facility at Ansty was the open bed to test Python turboprops, construction beginning in 1945. On this bed the engine, with its contra-rotating airscrews, was carried on a dummy wing specially designed

Test Site – 1955

to simulate the engine installed for flight. The bed (Number 43) was later supplemented by an enclosed and silenced bed for Python development (Number 44). The second step in the extension of the facilities was the building of two enclosed test beds (Number 41 and Number 42) for the 1,000 hp Mamba turboprop, intended for the Armstrong Whitworth Apollo and Handley Page Marathon civil aircraft and later for the Short Seamew spotter aircraft for the Royal Navy. The Mamba beds were later converted to Viper turbojet beds.

In 1948 the four Sapphire test beds (Numbers 45, 46, 47 and 48) were built. The compressor/turbine test plant (Number 40) powered by a 10,000 hp boiler and turbine from a Hunt class destroyer, was also built. The next extension of the test line was the building of a pair of cells (Numbers 51 and 52) for the development and pass-off of Double Mamba engines. Later, as the Double Mamba programme expanded, three more beds were built, including a dynamometer cell. By the late 1950s 15 turbine engine beds existed. A separate Small Engines Laboratory was constructed for the development of small air cooled diesels and the build under licence of the AiResearch designed auxiliary power units.

In parallel with the provision of turbine engine test facilities, manufacturing capacity was introduced and expanded. In 1949 what became Number 1 Shop, previously used in the assembly of Oxfords and Mosquitos

The new Engineering Centre

The entrance to the new centre

by the Standard Motor Company, was adapted to provide a production assembly line for the Python, by now scheduled for the Westland Wyvern naval fighter aircraft. When this production wound down, the 90,000 square feet of this shop was used for the initial batch of 28 Sapphire 6s. Some of these engines went to the US as prototypes for the Curtiss Wright and Buick built J65 version, others went to Switzerland and the engines for the prototype Avro Vulcan V bomber also came from this batch. When Python production and the first batch of Sapphires were completed, Number 1 Shop was used for Python and Double Mamba repair work and later for the repair of Sapphire engines from the RAF's Gloster Javelins. In 1952 Number 2 Shop, with a floor area of 70,000 square feet, was converted for the production of Double Mambas for the Fairey Gannet, Viper turbojets for the Australian Jindivik target aircraft and a first batch of Vipers for the Hunting Jet Provost trainer for the RAF.

With the decision to turn Ansty into a self-contained Engineering and Development Centre, Double Mamba build was transferred to Parkside. All development engine assembly at Ansty was moved into Number 2 Shop and Sapphire production was moved to Brockworth. At this time a further important extension was added by the building of Number 4 Shop covering some 100,000 square feet to contain a large sheetmetal development facility and a comprehensive development machine shop. The original hangar built

Sir Frank Spriggs opens the Engineering Centre

for AST in 1935 became Number 3 Shop housing the model shop, spares packing and the photographic department.

As part of making Ansty a self-contained Engineering Centre, a new office block was built. This comprised a design and production drawing office building and an administration block. The offices were built to Armstrong Siddeley specification by Kelvin Construction and the walling, assembled by Hawskley, made from extrusions and sheet supplied by High Duty Alloys. All three of these companies were members of the Hawker Siddeley Group.

At the time of establishing the Aero Design Office at Ansty, the Sapphire 6 was already in service. Sapphires 7, 8 and 9 were designed at Ansty and a project study completed for the Sapphire 10. Aero engine development by the Ansty team continued until some time after the cancellation in 1957, following the Defence White Paper, of the Supersonic Manned Bomber. This was the year of Sputnik 1, the beginning of the Space Race. It was also the year in which Sir Frank Spriggs, Chairman of the Hawker Siddeley Group, somewhat ironically opened the new Engineering Centre at Ansty. The dedication stone at the entrance to the foyer looked rather like a tombstone and indeed, one of the senior Siddeley engineers observed wryly at the time that it ought to have been inscribed "In memory of those who gave their lives to Armstrong Siddeley".

CHAPTER EIGHT

The ten thousand horsepower rig

It had not been possible to calculate by theory alone how an aerofoil would perform in a stream of air. The development of bladed components of an engine had therefore to be an empirical business, supported by theory, and depending on research, both on cascades of blades and on experimental turbomachinery in single or multiple stages. In the all important case of axial compressors, the key to good performance was matching of successive stages. Rather than by tests on the engine, this was achieved sooner and cheaper by rig tests on the complete compressor. But the power to test the larger compressors at their design point was prohibitively large. The ASX compressor, for example, had been tested at the Northampton Power Station where a spare steam turbine was available. At Parkside, in the early days, only limited resources were available and so the Company decided to build a major aerodynamics facility at Ansty. The plant was designed to test both compressors and turbines of full engine size using a steam turbine and boiler nominally of 10,000 output horsepower which had been taken from a Hunt Class destroyer.

So that power requirements would be within reasonable bounds, a compressor would be run at reduced mass flow and therefore at reduced pressure. Pressure at inlet could be reduced, thereby simulating actual service conditions at altitude, the power absorbed decreasing with reducing inlet density. It was thus possible to test compressors which would have absorbed much more than 10,000 hp at sea level. The compressor test cell itself was a 10 foot diameter chamber, the forward end of which formed a removable door, whereby the test compressor could be installed.

Turbines were tested by using a compressor to suck air through them. By running the turbines thus on air at ambient temperature new forms of blading could quickly be made from materials that were easy to machine. If it were necessary to examine the effects of operation at higher temperature, air from the compressor delivery could be ducted back to mix with air at entry to the turbine. Provision was made for further increase in temperature by the facility to include a combustion chamber in the ducting. The maximum power of which the dynamometer system was capable was 4,000 hp.

Steam for the compressor drive rig came from the oil-fired naval boiler with a steam raising capacity of 100,000 pounds an hour at 650°F. and 300 pounds per square inch. Steam could be raised in two and a half to three hours from cold. The high pressure (hp) and low pressure (LP) turbines were coupled in a marine gearbox, the output of which provided drive via a speed increasing gearbox, alternative gears being available to suit the speed requirement of the particular compressor. The LP turbine exhausted into a condenser which was cooled by some 9,000 gallons a minute of water from a 600,000 gallon artificial lake. The water flowing back into the lake through sprayers producing a multiplicity of fountains and, in adverse wind conditions, a soaking for the occasional passer-by, was one of the memorable features of the Ansty scene.

An indication of the complexity of the plant is shown by the illustration. The facility turned out to be a most valuable development tool. Notably an uprated Mamba compressor and a series of Sapphire compressors were developed by its use.

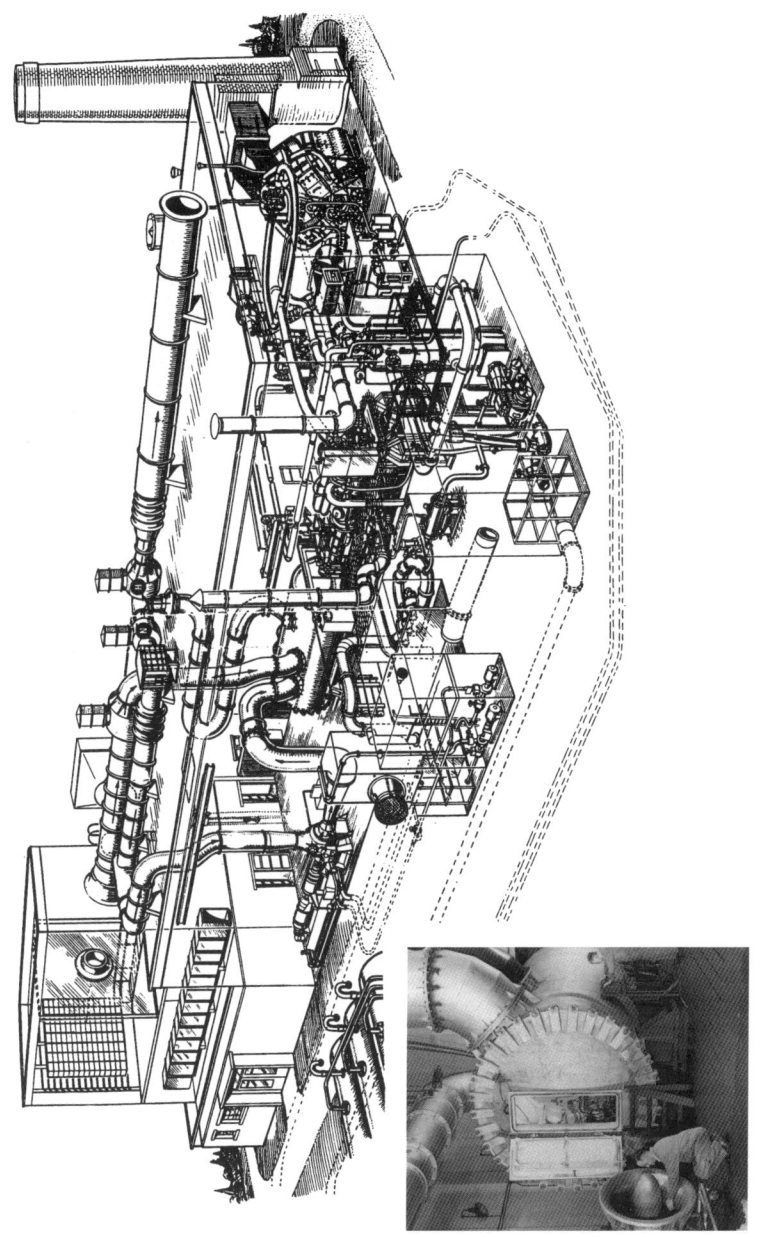

The 10,000 HP rig with its compressor cell

CHAPTER NINE

P176, a supersonic turbojet

By the end of World War II, the RAF possessed in Bomber Command an extremely potent military machine and the achievements of the Command had a major effect on post-war RAF policy. The American atom bombs on Hiroshima and Nagasaki endorsed the idea that the heavy bomber had become the dominant weapon. At this time the government once more made the assumption that it was unlikely that a further World War would break out within ten years. The RAF, therefore, replaced its Lancasters by unpressurised, piston-engined Lincolns, whilst planning for the longer term advanced jet bombers capable of more than twice the speed and twice the altitude of the Lincoln.

The outcome of these plans was the V Bomber force but in 1954, before they had arrived, an operational requirement was announced calling for a further considerable advance specifying a cruise Mach number of 2.5 and a capability of reaching 60,000 feet at 1,000 miles from base with a minimum range of 5,000 miles. This very ambitious specification had emerged not only ahead of the arrival of the swept wing V bombers but also ahead of the operational use of any supersonic fighter. New materials and new engines were needed. By May 1955 Avro had submitted in response its detailed proposal for the 730 aircraft and a contract was awarded in the summer. The engines were to be four AS P159 turbojets. The project design of these engines had been carried out at Parkside but, to reach its final form, the 730 had undergone a number of major design changes and instead of four P159 engines the aircraft was to have eight P176 engines with four in each of two rectangular nacelles, each of the latter having a movable centre body intake. The design work on the P176 was carried out at Ansty under the leadership of H S Rainbow. The shape of the 730 was to become familiar when, in 1962, the Bristol Type 188 research aircraft flew. Powered by two de Havilland Gyron Juniors, the Type 188 was a scale model of the Avro intended for general research at Mach 2 plus.

Intake pressure for the engines of the 730 was to be recovered for each group of four engines by a double shock intake. The engine had a ten-stage axial compressor, an annular combustor and a two-stage turbine. Operation at supersonic speed required limited thrust boost by reheat using a simple flame holder attached to the exhaust centre-body.

A novel combustion system reduced the length of the rotor so that it could be supported on only two bearings without risk of excessive bowing on shutdown. Although by the standards of the 1980s so short a combustor

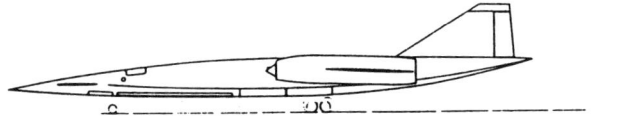
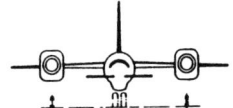

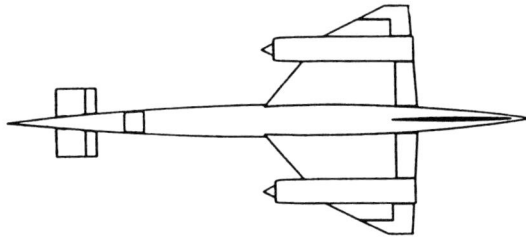

The Avro 730

would not be exceptional, conventional combustion chambers of the 1950s were much longer, requiring three-bearing articulated main shafts. At take-off with reheat, design turbine inlet temperature was 1400°K at a pressure ratio of 7.25:1. At this condition the thrust was 19,400lb from an engine of only 40 inches diameter. At Mach 2.5 and 60,000 feet, turbine inlet temperature was 1300°K and the compressor ratio 3.9:1. Most of the compression occurred at this flight condition in the intake. With the predicted 75% pressure recovery the pressure ratio across the intake alone was to be 13:1. The engine was designed to operate with a fixed throat area propelling nozzle under non-reheat conditions. Reheat was to be available for take-off

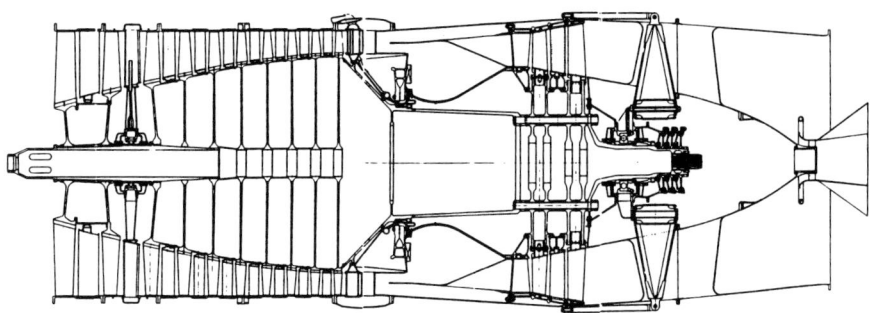

P176 Mk 5 sectional arrangement

and climb and in this mode, the turbine entry temperature was allowed to rise even though some increase in propelling nozzle throat area was scheduled. The compressor was within the state of the art in that average stage temperature rise was limited to 25°C.

The real technical challenge lay in achieving acceptable combustor performance within a diameter limited by the turbine and a length very much shorter than was contemporary practice. To achieve sufficiently rapid mixing of fuel and air, fuel was to be sprayed onto a rotating disc emerging as a thin sheet of liquid to be broken up by the air from the compressor. This departed from the rule obeyed by most combustion engineers that no moving parts be allowed within the chamber and it caused considerable difficulties in development. Furthermore, no attempt was made to mix by the conventional method of introducing dilution air through holes in the walls of the flametube, the products of combustion passing unmixed into the turbine nozzles through a system of adjacent radial chutes alternately carrying side by side hot gas from the burning process and relatively cool air from the compressor. The nozzles were to be cooled by being sited in the wake of the chutes carrying cool air. Mixing with hot gas was to be achieved within the nozzle passages in the centrifugal field induced in them. Thus the combustor itself consisted of little more than a primary zone. A combustor development programme was started using test plant at the National Gas Turbine Establishment (NGTE) and it soon appeared that the achievement of a steady flame might well not be possible and alternative schemes without a rotating disc were quickly on the drawing board. From investigations in curved passages made some years later, it was found that adequate mixing of adjacent hot and cold streams could have been achieved but with an unacceptably high pressure loss.

The programme came to an abrupt end with the publication of the Sandys' White Paper of April 1957 which called for the abandonment of manned bombers and their replacement by ballistic missiles. As the paper had it, "It must be frankly recognised that there is at present no means of providing adequate protection for the people of this country against the consequences of an attack with nuclear weapons. This makes it more than ever clear that the overriding consideration in all military planning must be to prevent war rather than to prepare for it" and "Having regard to the high performance and potentialities of the Vulcan and Victor medium bombers and the likely progress of ballistic rockets and missile defence, the government have decided not to go on with the development of a supersonic manned bomber, which could not be brought into service in much under 10 years". Had the bomber survived and the P176 with it, there can, however, be little doubt that the solution of the combustion problem within the given envelope, would have been an extremely difficult task. Referring to the demise of the P176, the issue of 'Flight' of 26 July, 1957, pointed out that "The engine naturally had the utmost priority and Armstrong Siddeley assigned to it virtually their entire research and development strength. Without prior notice, the whole programme was cancelled early this year, when the engine was in the hardware stage. This unhappy history inevitably delayed the Company's reappraisal of existing markets and prevented them from having a ready-made entry to the commercial field".

In May of that year, Elaine Burton the Labour Member for Coventry South, asked the Minister of Supply in the Commons about the effect of the defence cuts on Armstrong Siddeley. The Minister, Aubrey Jones, replied, "The cancellation of the supersonic bomber involves the cancellation of the defence contract for its engine. This, together with some running down in other work, will bring the firm's turnover down to about two-thirds of last year's figure. There is little likelihood of my being able to find alternative work to fill this gap…"

By February of the following year the Coventry Evening Telegraph reported a speech made by H T Chapman under the heading "Siddeley Recover from Body Blow – Chairman foresees full employment for at least three years". Speaking at the Apprentice Association Dinner he said that he was being "very cautious" in prophesying future success. He added, "Unless our figures are wrong, I think we are going to employ all the facilities and all the people we have now for at least three years. I hope it will be better than that". Before the cuts came he said, the firm had cleared its decks to take on a huge government contract for supersonic bomber engines. He believed it was the biggest contract of its kind ever placed by the government. Then came the White Paper bombshell. "I suppose of the five major aero-engine concerns in this country we have had the roughest deal. We not only lost the biggest and most important contract but we also had our development work cut severely. So nine to ten months ago you could have had my job for three ha'pence but you don't live in engineering by getting your tail down". He recalled that at the end of the war in 1946 the firm was employing just over 4,000 people and it had "no future whatever". But in the following ten years it had multiplied its turnover nine times. By April 1957 its payroll was 12,700. "We were literally bursting at the seams. We could always have more projects than we could successfully deal with" said Mr Chapman. But the firm had made one mistake, he said, too much emphasis had been put on government work and on aero engines in particular. He went on to outline some of the projects that had been put in hand to counteract the drastic effects of the defence cuts. The Company had decided, using its own money, to try to capture the semi-light aero engine market in the 1,000 hp class with turboprop engines (P181 and P182). "We realised from market surveys that there was a tremendous opportunity in this class, although we have at least three competitors. We cannot get government money to support us but I have got a considerable sum from the Group (Hawker Siddeley Group) to do it as a private venture. We are trying to stay, and will stay, in the productive lucrative line, which is the aero engine industry". In addition to doing a lot of subcontract work, the firm was making the Viper engine – a business which looked promising. (30 years after completion of its design the Viper was producing an annual turnover in excess of £30m).

The prospects for a T100 automotive project at this time also looked healthy. A major project already taken on by the firm was the 1,200 hp high speed Maybach Diesel which it hoped to produce for British Railways.

CHAPTER TEN

P181 AND P182 – the last of the line

In 1957 and 1958 H S Rainbow's project team at Ansty designed two new turboshaft engines, the P181 designed for helicopters and installations such as Short Take-off and Landing (STOL) aircraft with interconnected propellers and P182 intended for conventional fixed wing aircraft. The engines were to be developed in parallel using common components wherever possible. The main gas path components were identical.

Air was drawn through an annular intake into a combined axial/centrifugal compressor. Two axial stages with unshrouded blades mounted on annular discs were welded to a steel shaft on the rear of which was mounted a light alloy centrifugal impeller. Stator blades were located in the upper and lower half casings and immediately downstream of the impeller was a ring of diffuser vanes. After passing through the compressor and the diffuser the air entered an annular combustor. This was considerably foreshortened by arranging it as a reverse flow system. Primary air entered the combustion zone through vaporisers of the Armstrong Siddeley type. Secondary air entered the flametube via boss-like holes and tertiary air was admitted through simple holes in the flametube walls. The main fuel burners, together with the atomisers and igniters needed for starting, were mounted at the rear face of the chamber. The products of combustion turned through 180° to pass

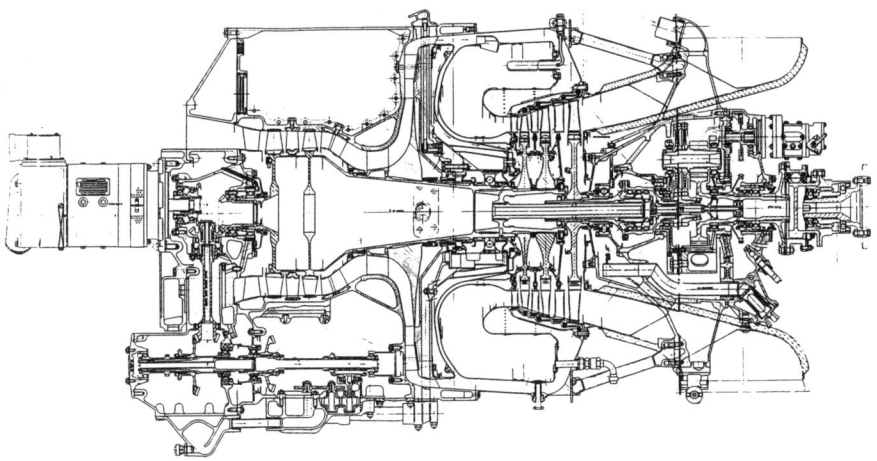

P181 general arrangement

through a two-stage turbine directly connected to the compressor. Downstream of the two-stage compressor turbine was a single stage free power turbine which provided output power driving a reduction gear at the front end of the engine. The reduction gear was contained within the centre body of the air intake assembly. A rear drive version of P181 was designed with the reduction gear located in the centre of the exhaust ducting. The exhaust passed to atmosphere through either a single, bifurcated or branched duct system depending on the type of installation.

Much emphasis was placed on safety in the event of engine failure by providing a maximum fail safe capability. This included a rotor governor and torque limiter on P181 whereby constant aircraft rotor speed would be achieved with the limiter to prevent excessive torque being applied to the rotor transmission system. The centrifugal compressor had overlapping steel diffuser vanes of thick section to retain significant pieces of debris, should the centrifugal impeller fail. The danger of a runaway turbine on P181 was reduced by a freewheel between the compressor turbine and the free power turbine. In the case of P182 an emergency control was operated by the power turbine to prevent overspeed. In both engines a double layer steel turbine stator casing was provided to contain a turbine blade failure and some further protection was afforded by the combustor which completely surrounded the turbine wheels. In the compressor casing of each engine, steel rings were inserted in the alloy casing in order to contain blades.

In general, the design of these engines was relatively simple. Stresses in the compressor and the reduction gear were comparatively low and all the mainshaft bearings were of ample capacity. The wide chord, axial compressor blades were less sensitive to the effects of deposits from atmospheric pollution, steel being used to minimise damage from the ingestion of foreign bodies. Reduction gearing was generously proportioned to ensure reliability and to extend overhaul intervals.

Development was undertaken at high priority, it being expected that engines would first be available for prototype aircraft by mid-1959 with production deliveries starting towards the end of 1960. Early test runs were not encouraging and it became clear that the swan-neck between the exit of the axial compressor stages and the eye of the centrifugal compressor was too short. The resulting bias of the inlet velocity profile made efficient operation of the centrifugal stage impossible. Though work continued for a while, the engine was finally abandoned in favour of the Gnome which, built under licence from General Electric (GE) in America, had come into the Bristol Siddeley product line with the acquisition of de Havilland. Thus the P181 and P182 did not long survive the merger between Armstrong Siddeley and Bristol Aero Engines and, though further aero engine development work continued on the Ansty test beds, this activity was administered from Bristol and Parkside and properly belongs to another history.

Responsibility for all aero gas turbines eventually passed to the Bristol team. At the time of the merger both companies had been in the development of gas turbine engines for applications other than aviation and the decision was taken to concentrate this work at Ansty.

Thus the Power Division of Bristol Siddeley came about and was set up under the technical leadership of W H Lindsey with F T Blakey responsible for the Commercial and Production activities. C E M Preston was in charge of Sales and Contracts.

CHAPTER ELEVEN

The high speed diesel

By 1955, when British Railways were considering the type of traction most likely to meet the requirements of the newly announced modernisation programme, experience on the Continent had already shown that for diesel locomotives of quite large powers, hydraulic transmission could compete successfully with electric transmission. It was therefore decided that this possibility should be explored and that Western Region, the erstwhile Great Western Railway, should take the initiative. The 2,100 hp V200 Diesel Hydraulic Locomotive of the German Federal Railways, with its exceptionally high power to weight ratio, had proved to be well suited to the closely knit railway system in that country. The relatively short intervals between stops and frequent speed restrictions were also typical of conditions in the UK. The demand for high acceleration to maintain the required traffic density in these circumstances would clearly best be met by lightweight locomotives like the V200 and had its loading gauge been suitable, this locomotive would have been purchased and put straight into service. As it was, the V200 was too high and too wide to fit the British railway loading gauge, so an Anglicised version was designed at the Railway Workshops at Swindon. The transmissions and bogies, except for the wheel diameter, were to be exactly as those of the V200. The V12 Maybach engine was therefore chosen. At the time, the relative merit of high and medium speed diesels for rail traction was very much a disputed matter but the success of the Maybach on the German Federal Railway was a fact. In the light of hindsight it became clear that the first class maintenance facilities and the long diesel experience in Germany played an important part in ensuring the success of this engine in that country. In due course the D800 came to work on Western Region.

The recommendation made in the beginning by the Maybach Company, that Armstrong Siddeley be asked to take on the licence manufacture of their designs was resisted by British Railways on the grounds that ASM was too much involved in its aero engine business to give the job the attention it deserved, and the work went instead to another firm in the Hawker Siddeley Group, Brush at Loughborough. In the event, business within the Group was reorganised and the Maybach contract came back to Armstrong Siddeley. Thus, in December 1955, manufacturing rights for the entire MD range of diesel engines were renegotiated, Number 1 Shop at Ansty being extensively equipped with purpose-built machine tools.

The licence agreement included application to ship propulsion, generating sets and oil drilling rigs and although the main business was with British

Bristol Siddeley Maybach power – "The Bristolian"
Inset – Machining a crankcase on a Hille vertical borer

Railways, outlets were sought by the Power Division in other markets.

The Maybach Diesel was of rather sophisticated design, the principal features which distinguished them from the more conventional designs were:
- A forged single piece disc webbed crankshaft running in a tunnel crankcase
- Pressure oil cooled pistons with detachable steel crowns
- Separate cylinder heads with cast-in central combustion chamber
- Overhead camshafts driving six valves per cylinder via hydraulic clearance adjusters
- A combined pump and fuel injector for each cylinder driven by the inlet camshaft

Bristol Siddeley Maybach Diesel

These features were common to the entire range, as were the cylinder dimensions of 185mm bore and 200mm stroke. The engines were available with four and six cylinders in in-line arrangement and in 8, 12 and 16 cylinder V form. Turbocharged and turbocharged and intercooled variants were supplied. The Maybach Company, which had engined every tracked vehicle used by the Werhmacht in World War II, had become expert in the business of high power to size ratio and had applied this skill to their post-war commercial diesels. Compared with the run-of-the-mill diesel, the Maybach Diesel design was more akin to an aircraft engine and indeed there were difficulties in the early days of manufacture at Ansty. Our production people, who had believed that a diesel was somewhat of an agricultural implement, had to learn the hard way that it was not so in this case.

Tunnel crankcase with roller bearing crank webs

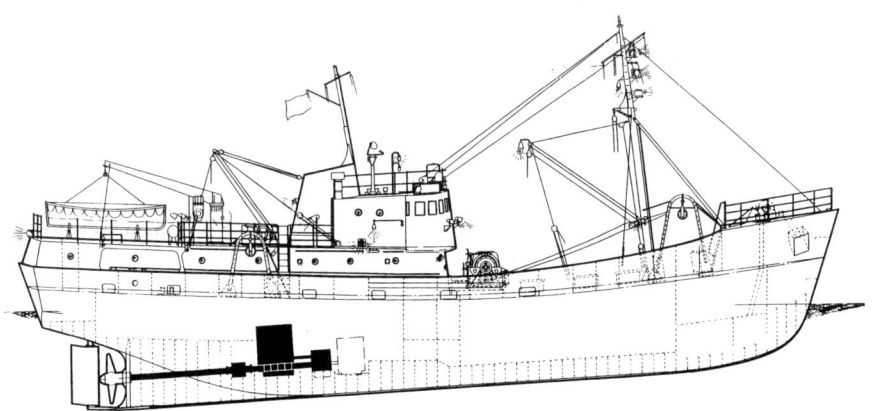

Small space needed by Bristol Siddeley Diesels

Of all the possible applications, perhaps the one least credible was that of trawler propulsion. In common with railway organisations the trawler operators were emerging from the steam era and the ideas of so sophisticated a prime mover were quite alien. Nevertheless, MT Blacktail, the first of an intended fleet of six middle distance sea trawlers, was launched in March 1961. It was powered by a pair of four cylinder MD 225 engines, turbocharged and intercooled. The vessel had a length of 115 feet and a displacement of 246 tons. Each engine had a rated output of 394 hp at 1,400 rpm giving a speed of 12 knots.

These small, highly rated engines, offered a substantial increase in cargo space and crew accommodation. In addition, a twin engine installation gave a degree of redundancy to cope with the case of engine failure. The drive from the engines was taken through traction type hydraulic couplings to a reduction gearbox, the output from which drove a three-bladed variable pitch propeller. A second output drive was connected to a DC generator to power the 115 hp trawl winch. Despite the advanced design of the ship with unusually spacious accommodation for the crew and the installation of the most up to date electronic fishing aids, Blacktail and its sister ships were not

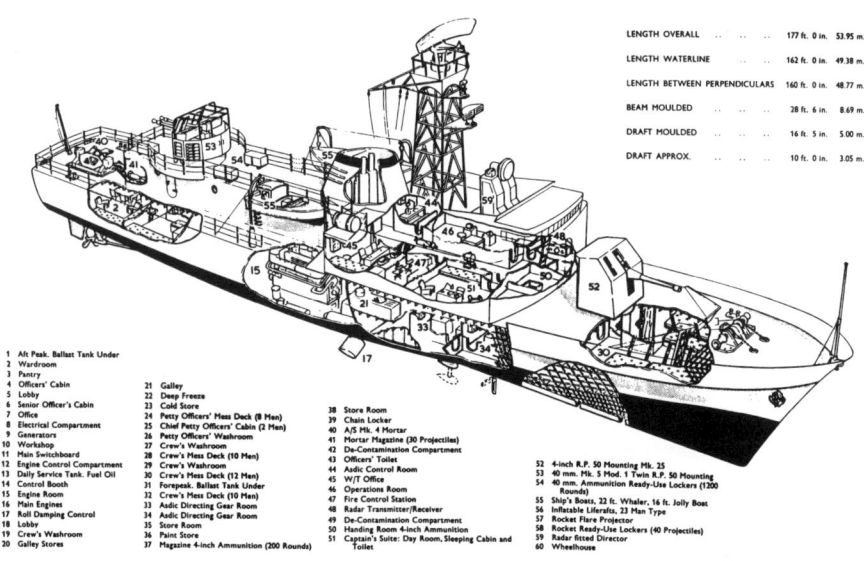

177 ft. CORVETTE designed by VOSPER LTD., in collaboration with VICKERS ARMSTRONG LTD. Powered by BRISTOL SIDDELEY MD. 872 engines.

The Malayan and Nigerian patrol boats

popular with the operator. Compared with the usual slow speed diesel, the MD engines were difficult to start and somewhat finicky. Exceptional care to keep the lubricating oil up to standard and the need to preheat the cooling water were unwelcome chores. There were no other trawler applications of the Maybach design in the UK.

The top of the range 16 cylinder intercooled and turbocharged V16 was sold to power high speed patrol boats for both the Malaysian and Nigerian navies. In this role they were very much more appropriate to the job and functioned well. Unfortunately sales were in penny numbers. The main market remained British Railways which, in addition to the D800 'Warship' Class, also operated the Type 4 D1000 Western Class and the Beyer Peacock Type 3 'Hymek' D7000 class. The decision to go ahead with the licence agreement and to invest a large sum in the production facilities had been taken in the light of an understanding about the level of British Railways' requirements. In the event, this level was not reached and the throughput in the shop eventually fell below the economic rate. Apart from a couple of 16 cylinder mobile generating sets for the Air Ministry, no other new business was done.

The scale of the High Speed Diesel project was very considerable and from the outset it was hoped that it would become the major breadwinner for Armstrong Siddeley, at first filling the gap left by the loss of the supersonic bomber engine and for some time thereafter even when work had started at Ansty on the Marine Proteus. From the outset, big business with British Railways seemed assured and a total commitment was therefore made to the project, including the massive investment in special machine tools. The size of the business set the project apart from other diversifications.

In the event, British Railways finally opted for much heavier locomotives with electric traction, but the sales of the Bristol Siddeley MD engines to BR had reached little more than half the number foreseen at the start. Unfortunately, the sales into other markets had not reached significant volume and so the Bristol Siddeley MD range went out of production.

CHAPTER TWELVE

Other diversifications

When the Managing Director of Armstrong Siddeley, H T Chapman, told the apprentices at their annual dinner in 1958 that the firm could find more projects than it could deal with, he was talking about the way to fill the gap left by the cancellation of the P176 aero engine. It was taken for granted that the special skills generated by the Company in the manufacture of aero engines could readily be applied to make other high grade engineering products. And so it turned out to be. But whether these would find a place in the market and make a profit was another matter. In those days market research was not too highly valued and product profit plans were unknown, or at any rate, unused. New products were taken on, more on an enlightened judgement as to their merit as a piece of engineering. The concept of the better mousetrap seemed to be accepted without much question. Thus Armstrong Siddeley and then Bristol Siddeley found itself in the business of diversifications such as automatic transmissions, reactor components, auxiliary power units, diesels, leadscrews and the like. But one by one these were dropped, the Power Division coming finally to the conclusion that it should stick to what it understood best, which meant changing course and concentrating on Industrial and Marine Gas Turbines. This road led forward to success but before so doing the net had been cast wide for other ways to generate profit.

SRM automatic hydraulic transmissions

In the late 1950s a licence was taken to manufacture hydraulic transmissions designed and developed in Sweden by the firm of Svenska Rotor Maskiner. The project was first taken on for shunting locomotives and its manufacture would have been complementary to the business of building diesels for rail traction. In the event, Ansty changed its mind and chose instead a version appropriate to heavy commercial road vehicles. The main advantage of the SRM transmission in this application was the fully automatic nature of its operation whereby the driver would be relieved both of the tedium and physical exertion of frequent manual gear changes. There was a good deal of evidence at the time of the benefits of so doing, especially where the driver had to concentrate fully on events outside the cab, as for example, in a fire engine or an aircraft tug.

The basis of the transmission was a torque converter in which the input shaft carried a row of inlet vanes forming a pump while the output shaft carried a two-stage turbine. Between the two rows of turbine blades was a row of guide vanes. These were mounted on a shaft provided with a brake. This shaft also carried the sunwheel of an epicyclic gear, the planet wheels of which were mounted on a carrier which could also be held stationary by a second brake. By selective application of the two brakes either double or single rotation was achieved. Thus, two levels of torque multiplication were available. Direct drive was obtained by a plate clutch which locked the input and output shafts together. An appreciable amount of hydraulic braking from the converter was available by applying the direct drive clutch and the planet

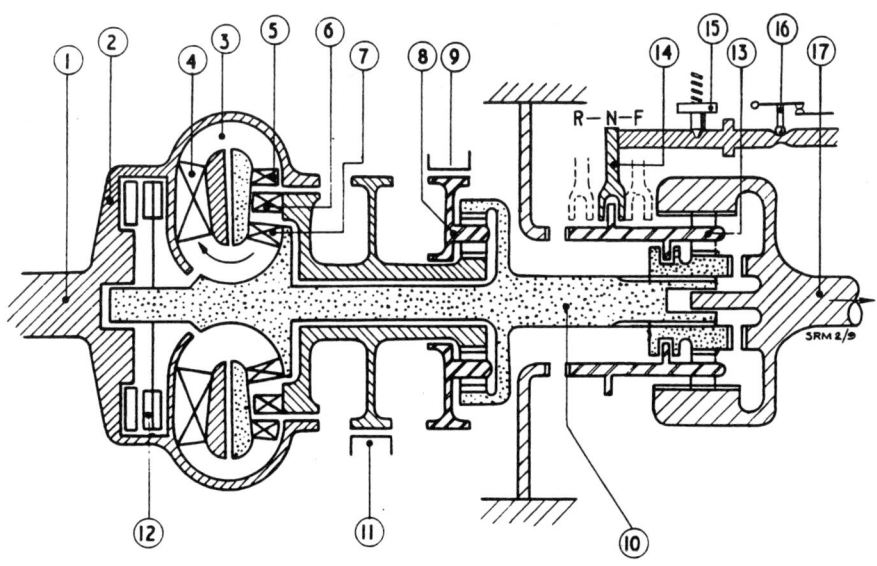

1	Input Shaft	9	Carrier Brake
2	Torque Converter Casing	10	Turbine Shaft
3	Oil Circuit	11	Turbine Guide Brake
4	Pump Vanes	12	Direct Drive Clutch
5	First Stage Turbine Blades	13	Reverse Planet Gear Carrier
6	Guide Blades	14	Forward-Neutral-Reverse Selector
7	Second Stage Turbine Blades	15	Locking Plunger (F/N/R Selector)
8	Epicyclic Gear Carrier	16	Micro Switch
		17	Output Shaft

BS – SRM hydro-mechanical transmission

carrier brake together, thus causing the guide vanes to rotate in the opposite direction to the rest of the converter. The change from one operating regime to the next was carried out automatically by a hydraulic autopilot which detected the ratio of input to output speed. The changes were regulated to suit both the vehicle load and speed and occurred at a lower vehicle speed for a light load than for a heavy one, thereby producing maximum economy.

By the mid 1960s considerable service experience had been obtained and much had been done to improve the disappointing early reliability figures. In an article in the Commercial Motor of August 1965 headed "From Cardiff to Edinburgh on One Foot" the test runs in a four-axle ERF heavy duty goods vehicle operated by Scottish Breweries were reported. The article pointed out that the cost of the box at that time was £850 but that it was "expected that this will be considerably reduced once output gets beyond the present pre-production stage… Remember that from this must be subtracted the cost of the standard gearbox, the clutch and the flywheel and the gear change mechanism; these together cost £338. This leaves £512 and if the savings in annual clutch replacements are around £45 a time the picture begins to look much healthier". But many automotive operators ran businesses on a small scale and first cost was usually the dominant issue. The promise of jam tomorrow was not a persuasive one. The real difficulty lay in trying to compete with the semi-automatic Wilson Self Changing gearbox which was already on the market at a much lower price. In the event, the investment in machine tools to produce the SRM box in quantity was judged to be not justified. When the project was abandoned in the early 60s, 36 units were in service including an aircraft tug at Heathrow, several units in Dennis and Merryweather vehicles of the London Fire Brigade and in some buses of Midland Red.

Ball screws and ball splines

In the later 1950s Armstrong Siddeley took up ball screws and splines manufactured under licence from Beaver Precision Products of Detroit, Michigan. Though ball bearings had had a long history in engineering, it was only with much later developments in precision production methods that it became possible to apply ball bearings to produce screw and nut devices for industrial use. Wherever linear motion had to be converted to rotary motion or vice versa, that is wherever a conventional nut and thread might be used and especially where frictional losses were important, the recirculating ball screw had advantages. In particular, it was able to operate at temperatures in excess of 400°C. with little or no lubricant. This capability was of first order importance in the fuelling system of a nuclear reactor and ASM were approached by the Atomic Energy Authority to consider only a production

The Bristol Siddeley 'Beaver' ball screw employs a stream of balls which re-circulate as shown in the illustration when either the screw shaft or ball nut is moved. The re-circulating balls and the screw threads in which they move are precision ground, minimizing friction and wear in converting rotary movement to linear motion.

The unique design characteristics and perfection in machining combine to give this ball screw a minimum efficiency of 90%.

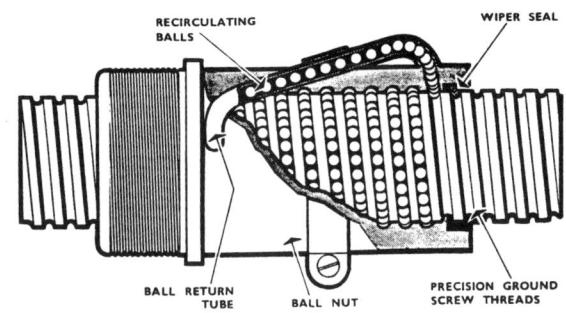

The Bristol Siddeley 'Beaver' ball spline assembly consists basically of the splined shaft and a splined sleeve by which the assembly is positioned as required for its particular application. Three or more equally spaced precision ground axial grooves or external splines are machined in the shaft and there are corresponding internal splines in the sleeve. Contained between the splines of shaft and sleeve are precision ground balls which remain in close contact and roll in re-circulating independent streams along the splines and return passages within the sleeve whenever there is relative movement of shaft and sleeve. The number of splines provided, will depend on the load requirements of the particular application using the ball spline assembly; the three spline arrangement illustrated is the ideal for load sharing, but designs are available with more than three splines to meet higher loading requirements.

The rolling movement of the balls in the specially contoured splines gives an extremely smooth relative motion of shaft and sleeve with almost negligible friction; this characteristic is combined with the assembly's capacity to withstand high torque and bending loads during linear movement.

In addition to the type of ball spline assembly described, there are also spiral ball splines available, giving any combination of linear/rotational movement.

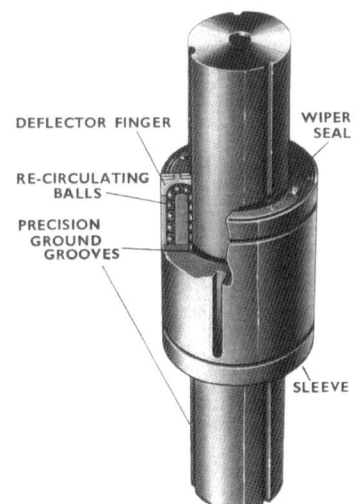

licence. In addition to their use in a nuclear reactor, ball screws could be applied to steam and sluice valve operation, to aircraft landing gear and to the actuators of the variable propelling nozzles of jet engines. In the conversion of torque to axial force or vice versa the mechanical efficiency always exceeded 90% and lead accuracies of 0.0002 inches per foot run were achieved. A range of sizes was made, varying from a 29 foot long version for the fuel system at Hinkley Point Nuclear Power Station to a screw two inches long and five sixteenths of an inch diameter.

Another use of precision ground balls was in the recirculating ball spline which resembles a conventional spline but in which the teeth of the mating splines are replaced by corresponding axial raceways in the shaft and in the surrounding sleeve. Each raceway had a row of precision ground balls with a passage arranged in the body of the sleeve for the recirculation of the balls from one end of the raceway to the other.

The licence agreement with Beaver Precision Products was made in 1958, the business as a whole being led at the beginning by Ted Wurr, as Project Manager. The design team was led by Geoff Barnacle reporting to Bernard Chatwin. At the height of the programme eight designers were producing some 20 design schemes a week. Included in the products sold were versions of a telescopic spline delivered to the Atomic Energy Research Establishment at Winfrith to shift the fuel rods in the Dragon Reactor.

In terms of profit the product was difficult to justify. It was finally abandoned with transfer of the licence and the more important tools to Precision Gear Machines and Tools Ltd., a subsidiary of Lear Siegler at its works in Bodmin Road, Coventry.

Small Engines Laboratory

To cope with the testing of a number of diversified products requiring relatively small facilities, the Small Engines Laboratory was set up at the west end of Number 3 Shop, in an area later to be taken over by the Bristol Engine Division administration offices. Four test cells were installed which were variously used to test automatic transmissions, auxiliary power units and several prototype piston engines. The latter included an uprated version of the Armstrong Siddeley Air Cooled Diesel, the project soon to be transferred to Petters, also in the Hawker Siddeley Group. Development work was also done in the laboratory on the T100 compound engine and on a pair of single cylinder Bristol Centaurus research engines.

T100, the compound automotive engine

In the wake of the success of the aero gas turbine, widespread enthusiasm erupted for the development of an automotive version. Such designs were mostly associated with a more or less conventional transmission system replacing the piston engine by the gas turbine. Already by the early 1950s prototypes had been road tested in the UK, the US, in France and in Italy but even though exhaust heat recuperation had been employed, fuel consumption was poor. Typically, six mpg would be produced in town and ten or twelve mpg on the open road.

In 1954, the Aero Project Office at Ansty, under the leadership of Horace Rainbow, began the study of a compound engine which would combine the high efficiency of the diesel with the torque characteristics of the turbine. The outcome was a design for a V4 diesel of 2.5 litres, the total shaft output driving the two-stage supercharger.

The exhaust gas from the engine was ducted to a multi-stage axial turbine connected by the gearbox to the rear axle of the vehicle. Thus the gas

T100 gas generator (V4 configuration)

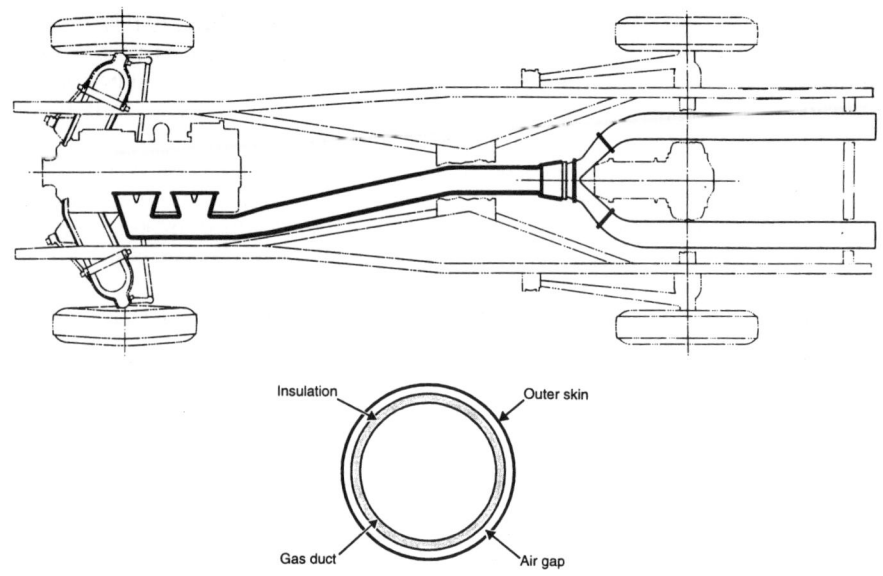

Section through gas transmission duct

T100 in Sapphire chassis (In-line 4)

generator and the turbine were mechanically independent. The unit was designed to give 200 hp and was originally foreseen as the propulsion system of the Armstrong Siddeley Sapphire Saloon. The test programme in the Small Engines Laboratory soon revealed two serious shortcomings in the gas generator. One was associated with the means of varying compression ratio with crank speed which was achieved by a movable junk piston automatically adjusted by a hydraulic servo. It turned out that the response to normal rates of change of load on the engine was not sufficiently rapid, indeed, this feature was replaced by a manual control for test purposes. To achieve a start-up ether was injected into the cylinders which produced some rather explosive starts and paroxysms of laughter in the test crew. The second problem was an associated one in that the topography of the junk head restricted the position of the fuel injector so that inevitably some of the fuel spray impinged on the cylinder wall. This produced an extremely smoky exhaust, so much so that Johnny Marlow (never at a loss for a pithy remark), who could see it from his office, at the other end of the Works, complained that it "looked like the Queen Mary coming up the bloody Solent". Analysis of test data showed that the expected levels of part load fuel consumption would not be achieved and that the proposed two-speed gearbox would have to be replaced in the vehicle by an automatic multi-speed box. Estimates had already shown that the gas generator would be more expensive than the equivalent simple piston engine. The extra cost of the multi-speed box made the whole project look doubtful at a time when fuel was cheap and manufacturers were shaving the pennies off production cost.

Attention was, therefore, turned towards the heavy long distance bus and truck market in which part load consumption was less important and where high power density would be more attractive. Gas turbine propulsion had been discussed with Leyland Motors over some years and a chassis was offered for a collaborative test programme. The problems associated with the cylinder head design were to be rectified by a wholesale redesign (T101) involving an opposed piston configuration instead of the Vee layout. In the new configuration each pair of opposite pistons were to be connected to a single crankshaft by a pair of rockers in the manner of the contemporary Commer TS3 engine. Variable compression was to be obtained by a relatively small shift in the position of the rocker pivots.

Analysis of the market prospect at this time indicated too small a level of potential sales to justify the additional development work and the project was shelved.

Air cooled sleeve valve diesel

When the demise of the Bristol Siddeley Maybach programme was approaching, proposals were made to use the diesel expertise which Ansty had acquired by planning for an alternative high performance piston engine. A diesel conversion of the Centaurus piston aero engine was one of several ideas. The case for the Centaurus was that it could be a very compact lightweight diesel with considerable attractions for both military and civil markets. The engine was in series production and together with its smaller brother the Hercules, had run over the previous eight years for an average annual time of over one million hours. Furthermore, these engines were then being repaired and overhauled at a rate exceeding 20 a month. From our point of view at Ansty it seemed that abundant service support would be available. It was proposed that the supercharged aero engine, which developed 3,150 hp at 2,800 rpm should be converted to a turbocharged commercial engine rated at a maximum power of 1,400 hp at 1,800 rpm. Preliminary design studies indicated that it would be more powerful than the 12 cylinder Maybach but at considerably lower weight and smaller size. Production costs appeared to be significantly lower than those of the German engine. The sleeve valve was an important feature which eliminated routine valve adjustment. It would be an excellent power unit, it was thought, for the propulsion of tanks. The proposal was enthusiastically endorsed by the

Single cylinder unit ex Bristol

piston engine development team at Bristol who saw an end to the mechanical problems created by the relatively high crank speed of the aero version. Ansty, though enthusiastic, was less sanguine, taking the view that low speeds were being exchanged for high firing pressures and that this would introduce new problems.

Two single-cylinder research engines were imported from Bristol and work began in the Small Engines Laboratory on two alternative versions of cylinder head, a prechamber design prepared at Ansty and a direct injection design from the Ricardo company. After 23 months of activity, the target levels of power and consumption were achieved but there remained a problem with build-up of carbon in the ring grooves of the junk head rings. This did not seem an insurmountable problem but Hugh Conway, the newly-arrived Managing Director, who knew a thing or two about piston engines, was such a difficulty. On reviewing the project he pointed out that Bristol Siddeley were really turbine makers and the Diesel Centaurus would be just one more diesel for a saturated market. Though he was prepared, he said, to be persuaded to the contrary, he thought Ansty should address itself to thinking five or ten years ahead with an advanced automotive turbine. The argument that automotive turbines were exceedingly fuel thirsty was countered by a recommendation to consider a compound engine. To that there was no answer. There was no further work in the Small Engines Laboratory and the diesel team was disbanded. One of its most able engineers, Bob Turney, joined the Ford Motor Company and became a member of their development team in Detroit.

Auxiliary power units

The increasing complexity of aircraft, especially following World War II, made ever greater demands for auxiliary power, both on the ground and in flight. Starting systems, cabin air conditioning, electrical systems and power controls often required separate power supplies. Post War developments in small gas turbines had improved reliability and safety, producing units of high power to weight ratio, of high mobility and which, as self-contained units were ideally suited to the role of providing this auxiliary power. They could be transported by ground trolley or mounted within the airframe.

In the process of searching for diversified products in the late 1950s Armstrong Siddeley negotiated a licence with the AiResearch Manufacturing Division of the Garrett Corporation of the USA to build a range of small gas turbines for these purposes which had been fully developed in the US. They were based on the '85' Series in which the major components were encased in a plenum, thus providing an envelope of relatively cool air rendering the unit far more convenient to use. The single combustion chamber was located so that it was readily accessible for routine maintenance of the igniter, the fuel nozzle and the flametube. The common control items such as the fuel pump, filter, governor and acceleration valve were combined in one casting thereby minimising the number of potentially leaky pipe connections. The design was well thought out and carefully engineered in every respect.

This diversification was very short lived, being overtaken by the availability of the Blackburn Turbomeca engines which had come along with the merger with Bristol. Thus the Palouste, the Artouste and the Turmo were marketed instead. The auxiliary power units were transferred at this stage to Parkside. In 1959 the agreement with AiResearch was terminated.

Reactor components

In 1956, as another diversification, Armstrong Siddeley took up a programme of research and development on gas bearings which was a continuation of work done by the Atomic Energy Authority. The activity, described as 'reactor components', included the development and production for the Authority of pumps and circulators designed for operation in nuclear power plants involving the use of gas bearings.

Though gas as a bearing lubricant had been proposed one hundred years earlier, the idea was of little more than academic interest until the start of the nuclear energy programme when the need totally to enclose pumps or circulators arose. In particular, it was essential to eliminate materials in the circuit which could form radioactive isotopes, thus prohibiting the use of oil as a bearing lubricant. Gas bearings could operate at extremes of temperature and had almost an indefinite working life, especially if run continuously. Furthermore, they were ideally suited to high speed operation. Pumps and circulators were of generally similar design, consisting of a shaft running in two plain sleeves, each of which was supported by a flexible diaphragm. The

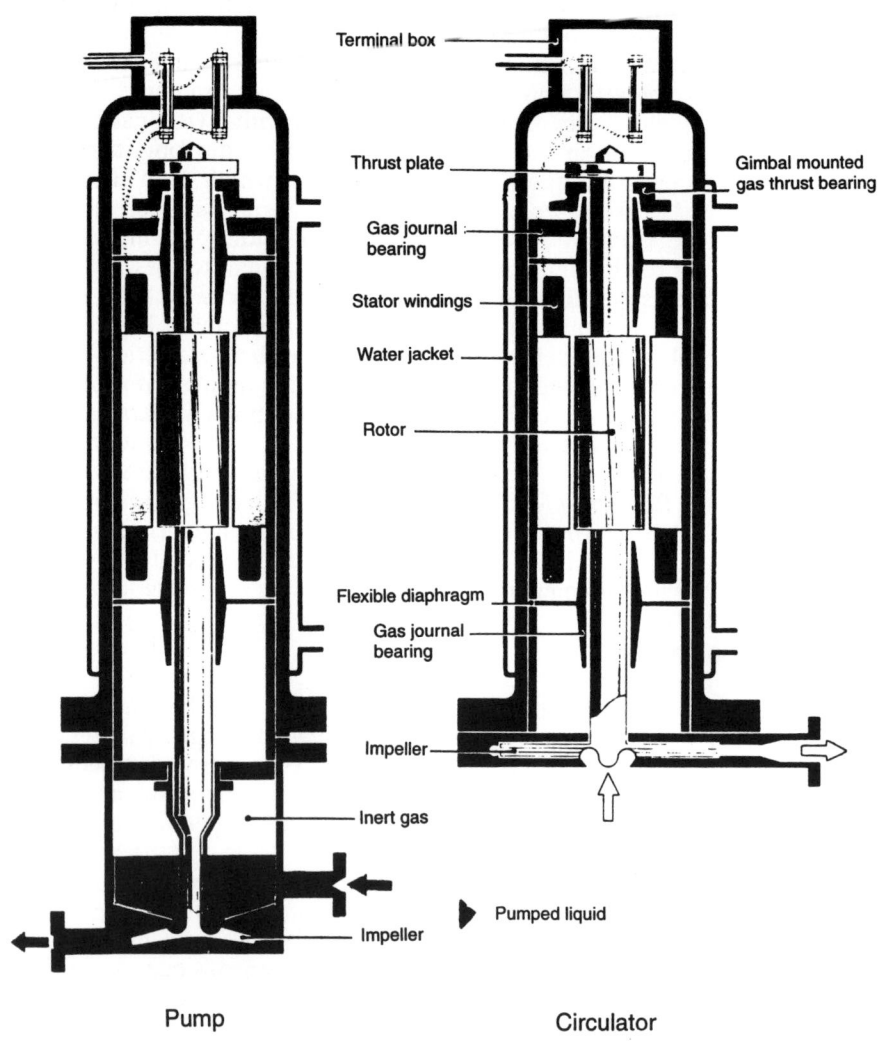

Diagram of pump and circulator

shaft carried an impeller at one end and the rotating plate of the thrust bearing at the other with the squirrel cage of an induction motor fitted to the shaft between the two bearing sleeves. The whole assembly was contained in a sealed pressure vessel.

Gas bearings called for considerable development skill and precision of manufacture. In addition, the manufacturing process required that the components were surgically clean and were not smeared with incompatible materials arising from the use of machine tools and from inspection, assembly and handling equipment. This need for the ultimate in cleanliness called for a special environment and extreme care during final assembly. No dust or other foreign matter could be allowed to settle on components at this stage since any such particles would be swept into the reactor gas circuit and become irradiated. A Clean Room was therefore built a Ansty. The running clearances were measured in tenths of a thousandth of an inch. Thus, although the bearing was extremely resistant to the ingress of foreign material in its normal operation, it was essential at the build stage to achieve the greatest cleanliness to avoid trapping even the smallest particles. The Clean Room was, in fact, a suite of rooms comprising three separate working areas, semi-clean, fully clean and ultra clean. Each was supplied with finely filtered air at closely controlled temperature and humidity. To minimise ingress of dust the pressure in the three rooms was maintained slightly above atmospheric.

The programme was beset throughout by difficulties. In the early days three very serious technical problems emerged: these were damage to the bearings during starting and stopping, half speed whirl of the rotor and excessive thermal distortion of the casings. Technical control of the programme was delegated to Brian Slatter and in due course he and his team put things right. A dozen machines ordered by the Atomic Energy Authority were delivered and ran year in year out quite satisfactorily. A subsequent order from Union Carbide in the US for a score of larger machines was not so successful and the contract was terminated prematurely.

On the financial side there were increasing indications that the business would not break even. Small production batches of machines whose design standard varied from one to the next made the achievement of profit very doubtful. Strenuous attempts to persuade the AEA to accept machines of common design did not succeed. The well known difficulties met by engineers attempting to satisfy scientists were frequently cropping up. Eventually the decision was taken by the Managing Director of Bristol Siddeley, Sir Arnold Hall, to abandon the business. Like other diversified products, this again was one well within the technical competence of the Power Division but one which eventually foundered by failure to secure an adequate market.

CHAPTER THIRTEEN

Rockets

Beginnings

The exceedingly rapid advances made by the Germans in rocket technology both before and during the Second World War, were without parallel elsewhere. By comparison, progress in Britain was negligible. Serious work had started in Germany in the years 1929-1930 by a few groups of private inventors and by 1933 this had attracted the attention of the Army Weapons Group. The major research and development station at Peenemünde was set up in 1937. Here activity was concentrated mainly on bi-propellent rocket engines using liquid oxygen for the combustion of the fuel. The development of large ballistic missiles was carried out, the V2 emerging as the only one to see operational service. Walther, working at Kiel, concentrated its attention on the use of hydrogen peroxide and also on this fuel in combination with suitable catalysts. Rockets propelled by the latter combination were extensively used by the Wehrmacht during the War. By mid 1944, the Allies had become acutely aware of German rocket development and especially of the Messerschmidt Me163B interceptor and of the V2 ballistic missile. Urgent steps were taken as soon as hostilities ended in Europe to interrogate German specialists and much of their know-how became available in the UK.

The involvement of Armstrong Siddeley began with its membership of the Lloyd Committee which first met on 22 October 1945 under the chairmanship of J Lloyd of Armstrong Whitworth Aircraft. This committee had been set up by Hawker Siddeley to see, in the light of the German progress, how they could best move forward to meet the requirements identified by the RAF for rocket assisted aircraft. ASM was convinced that the best way was to exploit German practice and proposed that a copy be made of a Walther 109-509 engine, which had arrived at Parkside towards the end of 1945. Early project work done by ASM on the Walther design was, however, frustrated by difficulties in supply of propellant which led to a change of fuel policy. At a meeting at Parkside in March 1946 the Ministry of Aircraft Production made it clear that the shortage of hydrazine made inevitable the cancellation of ASM's work on the Walther design. Armstrong Siddeley was asked to proceed instead with the study, design and development of liquid oxygen units.

ASM's idea of starting with a small copy of the Lubbock combustion chamber developed by Shell was rejected by the Ministry which preferred a more up to date model and offered to provide ASM with a liquid oxygen combustion chamber for preliminary tests. At the 1946 meeting the question of test plant was discussed, ASM pointing out that the work would be done at Ansty.

The tentative specification of the first Armstrong Siddeley rocket motor was:

Design thrust	2,000 lb
Life of Unit	10 hours
Easy ignition and reignition	
Propellant:	Liquid Oxygen and Kerosene

Electrical and hydraulic accessories to be driven by shaft from the main engine of the aircraft

An experimental feature to be included at a later date:	Variable thrust control from 100 to 30%

Reg Cleaver inspects the Snarler in tail of the Hawker P1072

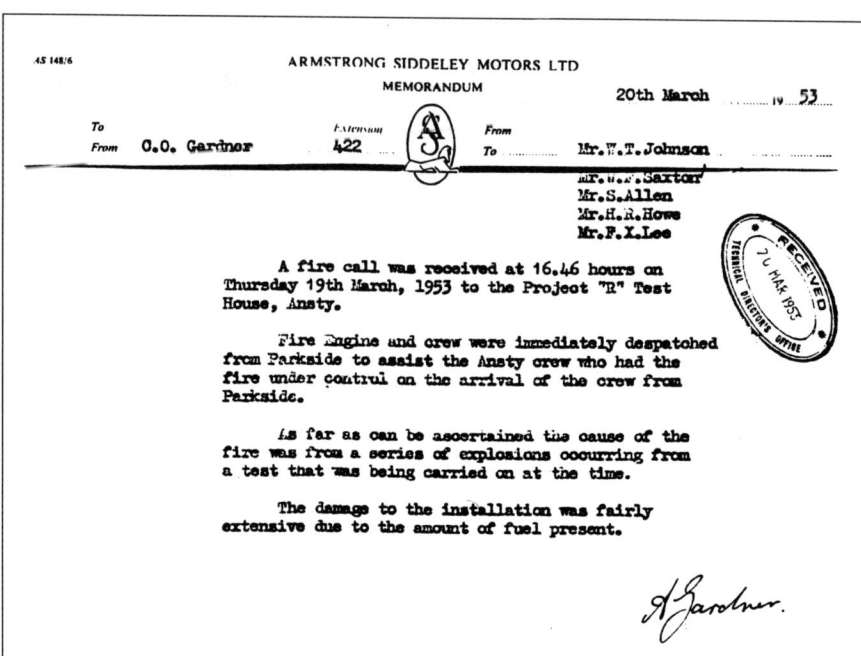

Fire in the rocket test house

In the event, Armstrong Siddeley's first rocket motor, the Snarler, used liquid oxygen and water/methanol as the propellant. This choice gave an optimum compromise between performance and durability of the combustion chamber. The great advantage of methanol was its miscibility in water whereby modest flame temperature was achieved. Snarler was installed in a Hawker P1072 piloted by Wimpy Wade and Neville Duke. It worked well and Wimpy was able to report from the first climb to 35,000 feet "It goes up like a bloody rocket!". In the presence of such explosive mixtures there was always a risk of disaster but the rocket activity survived all its years without serious injury to anyone, though as foreman Reg Cleaver remarked "We blew the roof off the Test House a time or two and we had some rather nasty fires".

The rocket business was, for most of us, always shrouded in mystery. The Test Beds, all but one, were set apart at the other side of the airfield and by the military significance of its work, rockets were always hush-hush. So the main line of the story is best told by Arthur Broomfield MBE who headed up the development side of Rockets from its early years.

Arthur Broomfield's potted history of the Rocket Department at Ansty

"I joined the Rocket Department, then called Project R, on 13 September 1948. Project R was, I believe, formed in 1946 as a small group within the Armstrong Siddeley Combustion Department. Sid Allen was the man in charge and he had working for him two or three Experimental Engineers and two or three Designers. I have no certain knowledge of exactly when people joined in those early days but certainly Harry Sunley was one of them in 1946, and I believe Dennis Hurden.

In the period 1946 to 1948 (before my time) the team was busy looking at various component designs for a rocket engine which would run on liquid oxygen and a methanol/water mixture. Typical activities in those days were designing burners which would mix these propellants, getting people to make a firework igniter and carrying out rather alarming ignition tests in a rudimentary sheetmetal combustion chamber. This latter test, for instance, was carried out at Ansty, the members of the team travelling out on a mini-bus at the beginning of the day and returning to Parkside when the work was finished. Sometime during late 1947/early 1948 the first rocket test house, No.50, was built. This was already in use by the time I joined the Company, when we were attempting to run the first prototype combustion chamber. It consisted of a plain inner shell sitting in an aluminium casting, split horizontally along its centre line and with a scrolled inner surface to provide the necessary cooling passage. This device was run initially from propellant pumps driven by an electric motor.

On 1 January 1949, the Rocket Department achieved autonomy from the Combustion Department (apart from its leader) and took up residence on the top floor landing of Number 2 Shop. We had three offices along the landing, one of which was the Design Office with Mr Hamm in charge and with David Andrews as his Chief Assistant. Then there was a main Development Office accommodating Dennis Hurden, Harry Sunley, Joe Gault and Tony Mottram. Next door was a smaller office containing one or two relative newcomers, together with a film reader who had a curtained-off enclosure to read the filmed instruments of rocket tests.

The site was comparatively quiet in those days (other people will know better than I what gas turbine activities were in progress at this time). Number 2 Shop, which was of course, an Aircraft Build Shop during the war, was sparsely inhabited by a shifting population of Standard Vanguard and Mayflower motor cars, since the space was still leased or perhaps rented by Sir John Black's Standard Motor Company.

During the two years 1948 to 1950 we were busy designing, making and developing the Snarler 2,000 lb thrust liquid oxygen/methanol rocket based on the earlier prototype work mentioned above. This was really a 'get the

Rocket site in the early 1950s

feet wet' exercise in rocketry, the final part of the exercise being the installation of the rocket in a Hawker 1072 for flight trials. The rocket consisted simply of its combustion chamber, propellant control valves both for the igniter flows and the main propellant flows, together with a gearbox, shaft driven from the wheel case of the Rolls-Royce Nene aero engine, driving the two propellant pumps. The rocket successfully completed a Special Category test in, I believe, late 1950, with Wimpy Wade or Neville Duke piloting the aircraft.

About this time we were asked to look into a rocket engine which would meet the Operational Requirement for a mixed power plant fighter. de Havilland Engines were doing the same thing, but we could hardly be said to be in competition because these were the days when the Ministry could cheerfully issue contracts to two firms to do the same job in different ways. de Havilland were looking at an Hight Test Peroxide (HTP)/kerosene propellant combination, whereas Armstrong Siddeley continued to look at liquid oxygen/kerosene engines. The final requirement was for an 8,000lb thrust engine and what is more, completely divorced from the aircraft's gas turbine. In other words, our rocket engine now had to have its own propellant operated gas generator and turbine driving the main propellant pumps. Liquid oxygen/kerosene has a rather high combustion temperature and we chickened out of trying to obtain the rated thrust using this propellant combination at stoichiometric ratio. In fact, we ended up with a real abortion in the shape of a tripropellant engine, the third one being water to cool the combustion chamber shell, the water being finally injected to keep the temperature down.

This concept kept a rapidly expanding team very busy during the first half of the 1950s. We did, in fact, get to the stage of developing a 4,000lb flight cleared version of the Screamer, which was due to be flight tested installed in a ventral position in a Meteor. This work was carried out at Bitteswell but before it could be flown the whole project was cancelled. Before this, however, we did a lot of work on the 8,000lb combustion chamber which was intended for the Avro 720 aircraft. This whole project was abandoned, however, some time in 1955 in favour of the SR53 mixed power plant fighter with the de Havilland Double Spectre in the tail. Before the Screamer work was cancelled, the sheer size of the job did cause quite a substantial increase

Gamma Series 201 rocket engine

in the numbers of the rocket team at Ansty. It also caused our second test bed to be built, this time in a separate and remote area on the other side of the airfield. This was Number 60 Test House, a reinforced concrete test cell and control room based very much on the 'sunken pit' type of facility, similar to those built by the Government Rocket Propulsion Establishment (RPE)at Westcott.

It was sometime about 1954 that the Rocket Department achieved complete autonomy and the technical staff were moved from Number 2 Shop into the three old Air Service Training buildings, still known to this day as B, C and D Blocks. 'B' Block was a Laboratory complete with an Electrodynamics Laboratory and Chemistry Laboratory on the upper floor and a Hydraulics Laboratory on the bottom floor. 'C' Block became the Rocket Design Office and 'D' Block housed the Development, Experimental and Research Departments. Sid Allen finally left the Combustion Department and became the Rocket Department's Chief Engineer.

In 1955 we were asked to get interested in the HTP/kerosene propellant combination so that we could develop the rocket engine required for the "Black Knight" high altitude Research Vehicle. This was to be based on a combustion chamber and turbo pump assembly already partially developed by RPE, Westcott, which in turn was based very much on German wartime rocket designs. The engine consisted of four combustion chambers running on HTP/kerosene, the HTP being decomposed catalytically by a bed of rough silver-plated nickel gauze. This fact alone meant that we had to augment our chemical staff and set up facilities for producing these gauzes, this being done in a Plating Shop across the road from the Laboratory itself in 'B' block. The fact that the rocket engine was now a vertical firing variety meant that another test bed was necessary and Number 62 was built in 1956, alongside Number 60, on the other side of the airfield. By this time we had quite a test complex built, with on-site Fitting Shop and Auxiliary Test Bed for testing gas generator pumps and turbines etc., together with a Surface Treatment Shop. The whole area also acquired a perimeter fence, complete with permanent Gate Police in their Police Box.

Soon after we started work on the engines for "Black Knight", christened the Gamma 201, we landed what turned out to be the major job for the Rocket Department, which was the propulsion engine for "Blue Steel". This was a stand-off bomb designed and built by A V Roe at Woodford, which in conjunction with the Vulcan Bomber came to be the main nuclear deterrent of this country during the 1960s. The engine, eventually christened the "Stentor" had two combustion chambers operating on HTP/kerosene with its own HTP driven pump assembly. The main boost chamber produced 26,000 lb thrust at altitude, whilst the small cruise chamber produced an in-flight controllable thrust in the range 1,000 to 6,000 lb. The initial development of this engine was started in Number 60 Test House, now free of liquid oxygen/kerosene development, and a second test bed was built at RPE, Westcott, on land leased from the Ministry. This was operated by a resident team of fitters and inspectors but with the technical control still exercised from Ansty with daily commuting by technical staff. The development work on the "Stentor" proceeded apace during the late 1950s and by (I believe) 1962 we had produced something like 165 rocket engines, 101 of these being production engines delivered to the RAF. The rate of production at its peak was four to five per month, these being built on a production line in Number 4 Shop, Ansty.

The area also housed a Rocket Machine Shop which did all the experimental and development machining required and, within its capabilities, sometimes production items in short supply. The main bulk of the manufacturing was, however, carried out at Parkside and by subcontractors. The Rocket Department from 1958 onwards found itself in its busiest and most stable part of its existence through until about 1965. In this period we were developing and producing the "Stentor" engine for the "Blue Steel" in continuing production quantities and had a steady line going for the production of "Gamma" engines of various versions for the "Black Knight" Research Vehicle. In this period 23 such vehicles were launched

Rocket test house

Production of Stentors in No 4 Shop

from Woomera in Australia, seven of which were fitted with a "Gamma 301" engine which was entirely a Bristol Siddeley design. This was based on the small combustion chamber and turbo pump assembly developed for the "Blue Steel" engine giving much higher thrust (25,000lb) and much improved reliability.

The next new rocket engine to come along was a small boost engine for the "Jindivik" target drone. I believe this to be about 1960, but it could have been slightly later. This was the PR37 engine run on HTP/kerosene again, giving 170lb maximum and throttleable to 50lb thrust, run from pressurised wing mounted tanks. The idea was to improve the high altitude performance of the "Jindivik" which was unable to fly successfully much over 60,000 feet due to the failing performance of the "Viper" engine at this altitude. To develop this engine we built the next test bed at Ansty, immediately adjacent to Number 62 test bed on which the "Gamma" engine development was being carried out and using the same Control Room which was dubbed 62A Test House. Because of its small size, the cooling of the combustion chamber using HTP/kerosene proved extremely difficult and the whole project gave us considerable trouble. Finally, it was flight cleared and three flight trials were successfully staged from Woomera. However, by this time the project was abandoned because of satisfactory improvements in the "Viper" performance at high altitude.

The next new engine to come along was the BS605 based on the "Stentor" small chamber and designed to give take-off assistance to the "Buccaneer" aircraft being produced by Hawker Siddeley at Brough. This was to meet an OR and an order from the South African Air Force to produce 16 "Buccaneer" aircraft to operate from their military aerodrome near Johannesburg. Since the airfield was at 5,000 feet and could be hot as well, some take-off assistance was necessary with a full load of stores. Somewhat to our surprise, the rocket engine turned out to be the preferred solution, both as regards cost and timescale compared with reheating the Rolls-Royce Spey engines. The resulting logistic problems which arose from this decision are another matter however. The development work on this engine was carried out mainly on our test bed at Westcott, including the installation of a chunk of "Buccaneer" fuselage modified to take the two retractable thrust units of the BS605.

In 1965 the first signs of a rundown in the country's rocket activities appeared. By this time the "Stentor" engine production run had finished, the end of the "Black Knight" firing programme was in sight and the BS605 could be seen already as a one off order, unlikely to be repeated. There was, however, yet one more major programme to come and this was the "Black Arrow" programme for launching research satellites into orbit. The "Black Arrow" consisted of a three-stage rocket with Bristol Siddeley getting the contract to produce both the first and second stage engines. The bottom stage engine had eight combustion chambers virtually identical to the small cruise chamber of the "Blue Steel" engine, but mounted in the engine bay in four siamesed pairs in trunnions and thus capable of giving full control in pitch, yaw and spin.

This engine was over 40,000 lb thrust and was mounted in a two metre diameter engine bay. Thus we found ourselves completing our biggest and last test bed at Ansty (Number 64) during 1965. This was again on the other side of the airfield, the site perimeter being extended to include it. There was great debate before it was built at Ansty since it was within a mile as the crow flies from the site of the new Walsgrave Hospital which was then being planned. We believed, however, that the bed could be successfully quietened (I hesitate to say silenced) by injecting enormous quantities of water into the deflector duct which turns the downward rocket efflux through 180° and away from the test cell. In the event, this was successfully done and I am not aware that we ever had any complaints from Walsgrave Hospital, mainly I

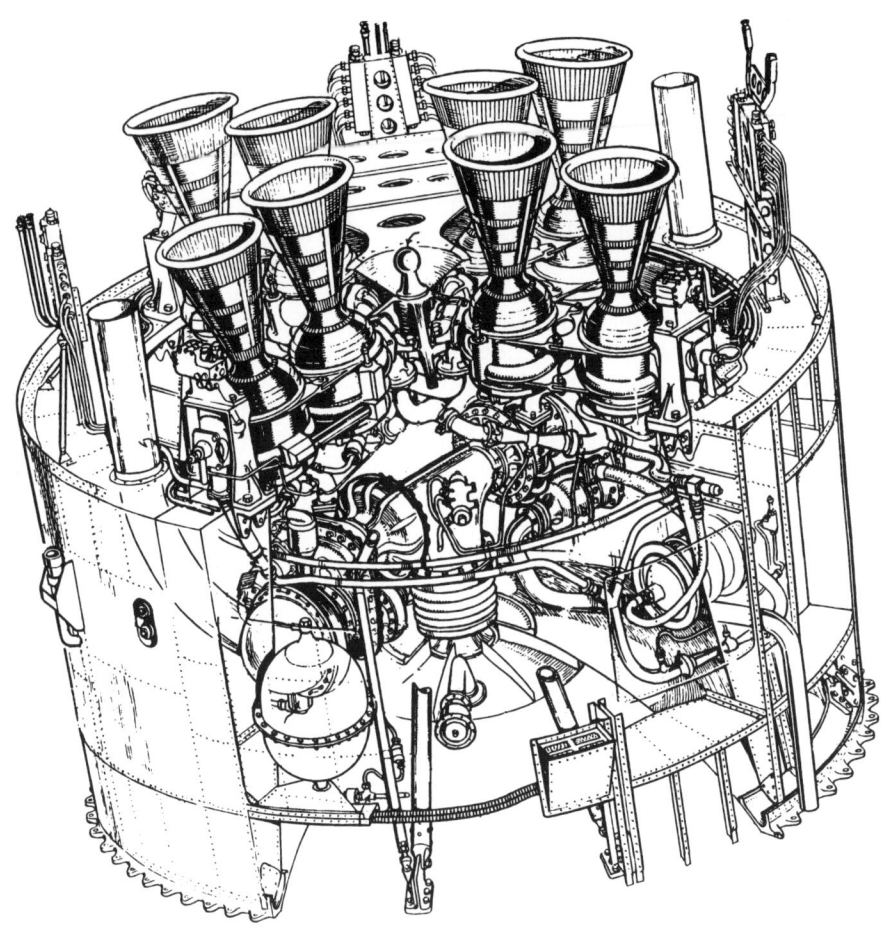

First stage Black Arrow

think, because tests did not normally exceed one per day and usually lasted for not more than 1.5 minutes.

The second stage engine of the "Black Arrow" consisted of two combustion chambers with a brand new turbo pump assembly, the two combustion chambers being each mounted on a gimbal ring so that full attitude control could be maintained. Work on these two engines for "Black Arrow" and on the BS605 was the main activity of the Rocket Department during the second half of the 1960s.

In 1967 Bristol Siddeley was taken over by Rolls-Royce and shortly after the rocket activities of Rolls-Royce were merged with our own. The Derby Rocket team had one main project, this being the RZ2 engine run on liquid oxygen/kerosene and was the bottom stage propulsion engine for the European Launcher Development Organisation satellite launcher. The engine was based on a Rocketdyne design but extensively modified by the Derby team. All their test work was being done at Spadeadam up in Cumberland, so it was only the technical staff who came to Ansty. I believe it was some time in late 1967 or early 1968 when we moved the technical people out of 'D' Block and formed a combined Rocket Headquarters in what was then the Apprentice School Machine Shop. 'D' Block itself became the Customer Training Centre.

In spite of quite strenuous sales efforts during the next two or three years, we were unable to start any new projects and the Rocket Department started contracting quite fast. The "Black Arrow" itself, with our two engines, was used operationally four times between June 1969 and October 1971. Only two of these launches were successful, but the other two failures were in no way due to shortcomings in the propulsion. This programme was finally cancelled in the autumn of 1971, although the final launch which took place on 28 October that year, successfully placed into orbit a research satellite.

Up to this time the ex Derby RZ2 team had continued their ELDO activities virtually unabated, but here again there were signs of reduction of support by the Ministry and the activities of the Rocket Department generally went downhill quite rapidly.

By the end of 1971 virtually all the old Bristol Siddeley activities had ceased and their members either left or were redeployed on to gas turbine work. Activity on the RZ2 was continued by the ex Derby people for about another year, then that too died the death.

CHAPTER FOURTEEN

Underwater weapons – the unseen activity

An overall survey by Nigel Ferriman

In 1959 the Bristol Siddeley Rocket Department at Ansty was invited by the Admiralty Underwater Weapons Establishment (AUWE) at Portland to study the propulsion of torpedoes by hydrogen peroxide and kerosene, thus making use of the considerable background in rocket technology accumulated by the Department. This high energy propellant combination offered a considerable degree of exhaust condensation and solubility with consequent reduction of exhaust pumping loss and thus enhanced thermal efficiency and a low torpedo wake. Various piston and turbine engine schemes and other propellant combinations were compared in this early work. Similar endeavours had been started independently by de Havilland at Hatfield in 1960. However, by mid 1962, de Havilland had been acquired by Bristol Siddeley and the combined team was thereafter located at Ansty.

During the winter of 1961/62 staff from the Rocket Experimental Office at Ansty were invited to witness and comment on the rig testing of propellant combustion systems at the AUWE at Weymouth. This was followed in the spring of 1962 by a request for practical help in running the AUWE test programme. Arrangements were made for the design and provision of various combustor, control system and engine components at Ansty. At this time the design of the "camplate" engine began at Ansty. This had seven cylinders axially disposed in a barrel arrangement around a central drive shaft, the driving torque being applied via a gudgeon-pin mounted roller bearing in each position to a two lobed camplate keyed to the shaft. Thus each cylinder completed two power cycles per shaft revolution. When finally available for test late in 1964, the design had already been overtaken but the limited testing served to show problems with the cylindrical rotary valve which was superseded by a conical valve in later engines. Useful design data was also obtained in other respects.

By 1963 the programme became focused on the provision of a powerplant for a specific lightweight, self-homing torpedo having a high speed, deep running capability. HTP/diesel was chosen as the propellant combination, although combustion developments were pursued with other combinations. Included in the latter were some highly reactive ones and it was quite an achievement of the designers even that they could be contained within the engine system. A propulsion system based on an engine cycle having an exhaust condensation/solubility capability was chosen as the front runner, the alternative being a very high pressure (above 3,000 psi) 'open' cycle engine exhausting at ambient sea pressure. Ansty was given responsibility for the latter. The design based on a three-lobe camplate was much smaller and lighter than the earlier camplate engine. Work both at Ansty and Weymouth continued during the mid 1960s on piston engines of this type. In 1967, pilot scale combustion work began on a "closed-cycle" engine design as a further option for the lightweight torpedo. This was based on a turbine prime mover and offered reduced noise and performance unaffected by depth of operation. A contract had been placed previously for the design and supply of the engine together with integral gearbox. The turbine, a single stage design, produced 350 hp and drove through a 33 to 1 reduction gear with helical teeth at 45° to achieve quiet running. Gas generators were made by AUWE and tested in 1968, the first engine going on test at Weymouth the following year.

By the end of 1968 thermo-chemical engines were dropped in favour of electrical propulsion for future British torpedoes. This contender had been highly competitive in terms of logistic considerations and of low self-generated noise. All work on the HTP/diesel camplate engine ceased. Work

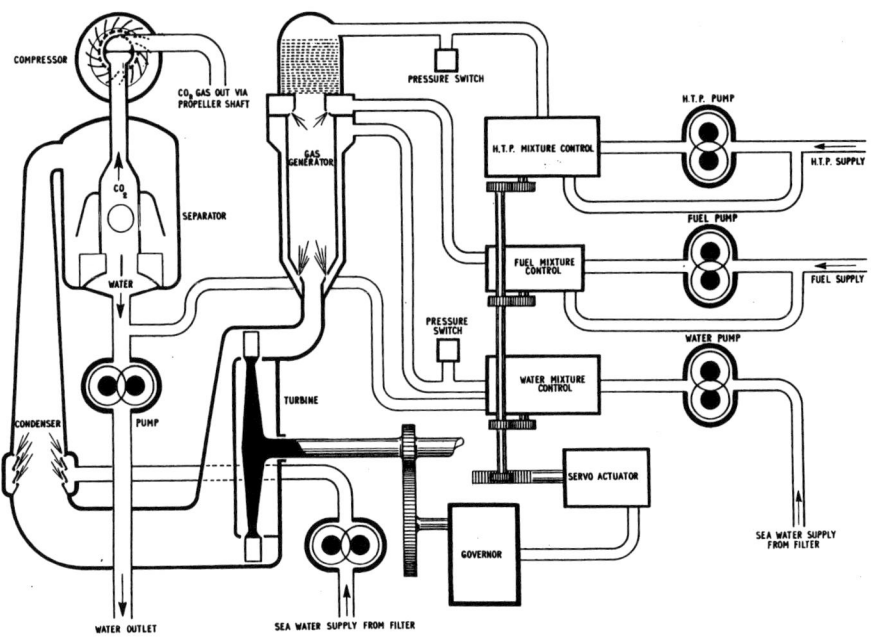

Liquid propellant system

on the closed cycle design continued through the early 70s and friction drives intended as a quieter replacement for the toothed gearing were developed. Considerable difficulty arose, however, with the accuracy in manufacture of the rollers.

In 1975 work on the closed cycle was also abandoned and the direct association between Ansty and the AUWE ended in 1977. What had been very much an under cover activity disappeared altogether and a programme which had lasted some 18 years and involved at its peak about 20 people ceased, though very few people at Ansty were aware of the event.

CHAPTER FIFTEEN

A merger and a takeover

In the springtime of 1958 the press began to speculate about major changes to the structure of the aviation industry. Following the Defence White Paper of the previous year it appeared that the long line of fighter aircraft was to come to an end with the English Electric P1 and that the heavy bomber would not go beyond the high subsonic, medium range Victors and Vulcans. In the civil field, the Viscount and the Britannia were finding a place in the market and the first Vanguards had been put into production. The Comet would continue to succeed in the market place until more advanced jet airliners came along. That was the idea.

Within days of the press reports the Minister of Supply, Aubrey Jones, announced in the Commons that "one had to reconcile oneself to some contraction" in the industry. He envisaged two engine manufacturers and three or four airframe makers. There were, at the time, five engine and 14 airframe makers. The Minister considered it reasonable that the manpower strength of the industry should reduce from the existing two hundred and fifty thousand over the ensuing five years to its pre-Korean War level of one hundred and fifty thousand. The message contained, however, some glimmer of hope that aeronautical research in Britain would not be allowed to wither away in the interval whilst the industry adjusted to the loss of military orders. The statement came as no surprise to the industry, Hawker Siddeley and Bristol Aeroplane already having agreed to pool their engine interests. Sir Arnold Hall, who was to become the Technical Director of the forthcoming Bristol Siddeley Engines Company, pointed out that the new company would "have at its disposal assets of £31 million and a labour force of 27,500". The resolve for the future was clearly expressed in a joint statement by the Chairman of Bristol Aeroplane, Sir Reginald Verdon Smith and Sir Frank Spriggs, Managing Director of Hawker Siddeley. 'This means' the statement went, "that a new giant of immense capability will take a place of leadership in the aero engine field, covering the entire range of turboprops, turbojets, ramjets and rocket motors". It was clear, nevertheless, that Rolls-Royce was still the larger producer but Bristol Siddeley had every intention of challenging that leadership.

In January 1959 the Ministry of Supply announced the placing of a contract for the RAF's new strike and reconnaissance aircraft TSR2, the work being shared 50-50 between Vickers Armstrong and English Electric. TSR2 was to be supersonic and also to have the ability to take off from small airfields with rudimentary surfaces. Taking over the role of the Canberra it would therefore be of much higher performance and of greater operational flexibility. The engine was to be a development of the Olympus installed at that time in the Vulcan bombers.

Bristol Siddeley at Ansty

The loss of the P176 had left Ansty with only one significant aero project, the P181/182 but with flourishing activities in diesels and rockets. In March 1959 S G Hooker and E Warlow-Davies circulated a letter to all aero personnel at Ansty. It pointed out that the contract for the TSR2 engines had been won in the face of intense competition from Rolls-Royce. The specification was the most advanced in the world and the job would be a mammoth task; a strong team was therefore essential. The P181 would be subjected to intense development and "it is our intention to fight with all the means in our power to get this engine established". As it turned out later, the engine suffered a major design shortcoming which would have been exceedingly expensive to rectify.

In July 1959 Bristol's P F Green addressed Ansty aero personnel writing "with Patchway chosen as the Aero Engineering headquarters, it is obviously uneconomic from the Company's viewpoint to have a large drawing office located at Ansty". This was the coup de grace for the Ansty aero team. The acquisition of the de Havilland Engine Company two years later bringing with it the Gnome finally put paid to the P181 and P182.

In 1959 the Power Division was formed at Ansty under the technical leadership of W H Lindsey. Ansty had become the last bastion of the Armstrong Siddeley engineering team which had already diversified into a wide range of high technology products. By the end of 1958 Armstrong Siddeley had taken on diesels, nuclear components, Beaver ball lead screws, aircraft APUs, hydraulic transmissions, the T100 and industrial and marine gas turbines. The emphasis in the beginning was on the high speed diesel and rocket motors. Little more than a decade later the general policy of diversification was to be abandoned, by which time Ansty was firmly established as a major world competitor in aero derivative industrial and marine gas turbines.

In the late 1960s a further structural change overtook Ansty, again following a governmental review. The Plowden Committee of 1964-65 had recognised that though the British aircraft industry had, over half a century, made a major contribution to the defence, the economy and the technology of the country, it had in more recent times suffered setbacks and frustrations. Earlier in 1965 three major projects, the HS681, the P1154 and the TSR2 had been cancelled. British civil aircraft of the new generation of advanced jets had, in spite of their technical qualities, not realised the commercial expectations with which they were launched. Plowden made recommendations for:

1. Wholehearted collaboration with Europe to evolve an industry capable of being fully competitive with the United States
2. Concentration on projects for which the development costs were not disproportionate in relation to the market
3. Purchase from the US where the requirement could not be met by a European project
4. Overhaul and improvement of the processes both in government and industry for making and selling aircraft
5. Purchase by the government of a share in the airframe companies

In the detailed conclusions relating to organisation of the industry, the Plowden Committee believed the main question to be whether the two existing airframe groups or the two aero engine groups should be merged. Such mergers would offer some advantages but no firm conclusion could be drawn. The decision would be deferred until the future workload on the industry could be estimated with greater confidence.

The report was presented in December 1965. However inconclusive it may have seemed, the writing was on the wall. Further consideration of the report and its implications was a factor in bringing Rolls-Royce and Bristol together for exploratory talks. Another factor was that BSE had recently entered discussions with Pratt and Whitney and SNECMA to explore jointly the possibility of working together on big fan commercial engines, a situation which posed a major threat to Rolls-Royce's own plans in this field.

Indeed, on 24 December 1965, Sir Denning Pearson, Chairman of Rolls-Royce, had written to the Permanent Secretary to the Ministry of Aviation about the engine for the proposed European Airbus in the following terms:

"Rolls-Royce with the encouragement and financial support of the British government, have for some very considerable time been studying and doing research and rig work into the optimum configuration of the next generation of large subsonic transport engines for both short and long range aircraft to replace the Conway. This work has recently culminated in the decision to build a demonstrator engine jointly financed by the government and the Company. In view of this work we would expect to be in a strong position to put up a proposition for a new engine for the Airbus based on the above work. We have reason to believe that our competitors, Bristol Siddeley, have not received a similar contract from the government in this field or carried out the same amount of preliminary work.

We are very disturbed, however, at the press report that in order to compensate for their lack of knowledge and experience in this particular field they are now seeking an association with our only competitor in the large subsonic engine field, Pratt and Whitney. We cannot believe it would be the policy of the British government at one and the same time to finance preliminary work on a Rolls-Royce engine and countenance an association between Bristol Siddeley and the main competitor of that engine. Quite apart from this, such an association would consolidate on a permanent basis the present link between Pratt and Whitney and SNECMA and in effect provide Pratt and Whitney with a firm foothold right inside the British and European market. If such an association led to an engine for the Airbus, it would be a Pratt and Whitney engine, as neither Bristol Siddeley nor SNECMA have the experience to make such a contribution to such a project.

This situation could, of course, be resolved if the British government were prepared at this stage to nominate Rolls-Royce as the British partner in any European collaboration on the provision of an engine for the Airbus. If it was felt essential a clause could be added to the effect that in the event the work would be shared with Bristol Siddeley…"

By October 1966 Rolls-Royce had successfully offered £63.3 million for the acquisition of Bristol Siddeley and by March of the following year the formation of the Industrial and Marine Division (IMD) of Rolls-Royce had been announced. The new Division was to be responsible for all marine and industrial gas turbines in engineering, marketing and product support. W F Saxton was appointed Managing Director, W H Lindsey Director of Engineering, F T Blakey Financial and Commercial Director, A H Fletcher Director of Marketing, A Jubb Director of Future Projects and R W F Farthing Director. About half the personnel on the site would continue to work on aero engines of Bristol origin and the remainder became members of IMD. Some key members of the Derby Industrial Gas Turbine Department were transferred to the new Division.

At this time the combined achievement of the new IMD amounted to the sale or ordering of some 450 Olympus, Avon, Proteus, Tyne and Gnome engines and a total export sale of £15 million.

IT was announced on March 1 that Rolls-Royce Limited is forming a new division to handle the industrial and marine gas turbine activities of Rolls-Royce and Bristol Siddeley Engines Limited.

The new division will be known as the Rolls-Royce Industrial and Marine Gas Turbine Division.

Its headquarters will be at Ansty, near Coventry, in the premises occupied by the Bristol Siddeley Engines Industrial Division.

The new division will offer a wider range of industrial and marine gas turbines based on aero-engine gas generators than any other manufacturer in the world.

It will have available for industrial or marine adaptation the whole of the gas turbine range now being manufactured and developed by the Rolls-Royce Aero Engine Division and the Bristol Siddeley Aero and Small Engine Divisions.

The division will be responsible for the engineering, marketing (including sales and service) and all the commercial activities in this field.

It will not manufacture, but will procure gas turbines (the Avon from Glasgow, Olympus from Patchway, Proteus from Parkside, etc) from the aero-engine producing divisions. In addition, the new division will continue the rocket activities of the Bristol Siddeley Industrial Division.

Commenting on the new division, Sir Denning Pearson, Chief Executive and Deputy Chairman of Rolls-Royce, said: 'The potential market for industrial and marine gas turbines is expanding rapidly and the new Rolls-Royce division will concentrate on satisfying this market.

We look forward with confidence to a growing future for this type of product, particularly in the export field.'

Mr W. F. Saxton, formerly Managing Director of the Bristol Siddeley Industrial Division, has been appointed Managing Director of the new division.

Speaking of the forward prospects, he said: 'I am confident that the Division has a very bright future. The combination of the products of Rolls-Royce and Bristol Siddeley gives us a tremendous range of engines, backed by a wealth of research, development and operating experience. These products do not clash, they are complementary and there will be an interchange within the Division of the knowledge gained over an extremely wide field.'

Mr W.F. Saxton

Other members of the Divisional Board are Mr W. H. Lindsey (Director of Engineering); Mr F. T. Blakey (Financial Controller and Commercial Director); Mr A. H. Fletcher (Director of Marketing); Mr A. Jubb (Director of Future Projects) and Mr R. W. F. Farthing.

Mr Saxton and Mr Lindsey relinquish their positions on the Board of Bristol Siddeley Engines Limited.

Top to bottom-Right,
Mr W.H. Lindsey
Mr A.H. Fletcher,
Mr R.W.F. Farthing.

Below.
Mr F.T. Blakey,
Mr A. Jubb.

Hs MEMORIAL SERVICE

A MEMORIAL service to the late Lord Hives and to other employees of the Company now deceased, will be held in the Welfare Hall, Nightingale Road, Derby, on April 26, from 12.25 pm to 12.50 pm.

The service will be organized by Derby Main Works Christian Fellowship and will be addressed by Mr Alan Swinden, Director, Engineering Industry Training Board.

From Rolls-Royce News – 29 March 1967

CHAPTER SIXTEEN

The fourth of February 1971 – the unthinkable actually happened

Long serving members of the aero engine industry quite understandably came to regard the future of the business in the post war years as somewhat uncertain. At Ansty we had met triumph and disaster and had survived. Within three years of establishing aero engine design and development on the site and with great promise of an expanding workload, the Sandys White Paper of 1957 came out and with it disappeared the Avro supersonic bomber. Almost all our energies had been concentrated on the P176 engine for this aircraft, a contract we had won in the face of stiff competition from Derby. The outcome was the shotgun marriage of Armstrong Siddeley with Bristol Aero Engines and as the newly formed Power Division, we lived to fight another day. We pressed on and established the fledgling industrial and marine business but within ten years we were swallowed by Rolls-Royce. Off we went again strengthened by the addition of new products and with an infusion of key people from the Industrial side at Derby. Thus we had attained a dominant position in the market and were far better able to take on the industrial and marine competition of the US giants.

Was it possible that by 1969 at last we could be home and dry? At the time, none of us questioned the inevitability of the RB211 as the means of ensuring the survival of the Company in the big league but clouds appeared on the horizon when one of our Lockheed watchers found in the 2 June 1969 issue of the US magazine Newsweek, an article headed "The crisis at Lockheed". The news was that despite its large backlog in orders for both civilian and defence work, the cancellation of an $875 million order for Cheyenne Helicopter gunships and Congressional investigations into Lockheed's C5A contract were causing great problems. Moreover, the L-1011 was under intensive pricing pressure from the other large airframe builders. A Lockheed executive was quoted as saying "We're on the canvas and the count is nine, but we're not out". Then in the November 1969 issue of Rolls-Royce News an article appeared under the heading "Our Company Faces Challenge". The message was that the rate of return on capital employed was less than the average for industrial companies in the UK. Redundancy was occurring in the Aero Division at Derby and, in the May 1970 issue of the News, profits were reported to be sharply down. We were on the sidelines at Ansty and there was not much we could do but get on with it and hope for the best.

The subsequent progression of events and the hanging of Rolls-Royce by a thread of carbon fibre is too familiar a story to be repeated. The axe fell on the morning of 4 February 1971. A message came instructing management to attend a meeting in the Executive Dining Room at 11.00 am. F T Blakey read out the following statement from the Main Board to the assembled managers:

"ROLLS-ROYCE BOARD STATEMENT

1. The programme of the RB211 engine for the Lockheed Trijet aircraft, due in service in November of this year has met with even greater problems than were foreseen in November last.

2. The consequences can be summarised as follows:

   − While the Board is confident that an engine fully capable of meeting the specification can be developed, the time required to achieve this will stretch beyond the time available under the contract with the Lockheed Corporation

   − The costs of launching the engine will exceed by a wide margin the earlier estimates on which the Company sought additional facilities of £60 million last November. None of this money has been paid; its availability from the government and Banks was made conditional on a satisfactory report by independent accountants whose work has not yet been completed

   − The earlier estimates of the production losses are expected to be substantially increased

3. These factors give rise to additional costs and liabilities which are wholly beyond the financial resources available to Rolls-Royce. In these circumstances it is not feasible for them to proceed with the RB211 under the present contract.

4. The loss of resources already committed to the project combined with the losses which will arise on termination are on such a scale that they are likely to exceed the net tangible assets of the Company.

5. In light of this situation the Board have decided that they have no alternative but to ask the Trustees of the Debenture Holders to appoint a Receiver and Manager.

6. The government has been fully informed.

7. Rolls-Royce is engaged on important projects affecting the government's defence programme; in addition there is the need to keep in service Commonwealth and foreign air forces and a large number of civil and commercial operations; there are also important joint venture projects in progress with certain companies in America and certain companies in Europe. The Board have had discussions with the government as to the best possible means of protecting these interests and it is understood the government will be making an announcement later today.

8. Whatever arrangements may be made it is unfortunately clear that substantial redundancies are inevitable. The Receiver will no doubt arrange early discussions with staff and unions. The Board is distressed by the hardship which will be caused to many.

9. The Board deeply regret the loss and embarrassment which will result from the failure of the Company to meet its obligations to the shareholders, to the Lockheed Corporation and to the banking institutions and trade suppliers.

10. The Board consider that the shareholders should be given an opportunity of having an independent enquiry made into the facts of the situation which has arisen. It has therefore been resolved to convene an Extraordinary General Meeting of the Company to be held as soon as practicable at which the members will be asked to pass a Special Resolution in accordance with Section 165(a) of the Companies Act 1948 requesting the Secretary of State for Trade and Industry to appoint one or more Inspectors to investigate the affairs of the Company and make a report thereon to the Secretary of State.

Possible question

It is anticipated that a question may be raised on the payment of wages and salaries.
In this event the following reply has been authorised:

"The situation is that all those now on the payroll will continue to be paid at their present rates.
All decisions regarding continuing employment will be made by the Receiver Manager but if in the future a decision is made by him that an employee is not required, then at the minimum, payments under the Redundancy Payments Act will be made".

It had taken two years from the first signs of trouble but it had finally come to this. One's recollection is that Mr Blakey's statement produced few questions, there hardly seemed much point in chewing it over.

One tangible impact of the collapse was that within days the heating went off. Our supplies of fuel oil had been exhausted and the purchase of new stocks was not immediately possible. We worked in overcoats.

On 22 March we received a telex message from Conduit Street, the London office of Rolls-Royce Limited:

"The government made an announcement in the House of Commons today as follows:

In pursuance of the government's declared intention to acquire such assets of the aero engine and marine and industrial gas turbine activities of Rolls-Royce Limited as may be essential for our National Defence, to our collaborative programmes with other countries and to many air forces, civil airlines and private operators all over the world, Heads of Agreement covering the purchase of such assets (the composition of which has not yet been finally determined) have now been signed between the Receiver, Rolls-Royce (1971) Limited and my Department, the government provides for payment of a fair price by negotiation between the parties to the Heads of Agreement with provision, in the event of disagreement, for reference to an expert assessor whose decision will be binding on all the parties.

With the signing of the Heads of Agreement, it now becomes possible for the new company to commence operations. This must, of course, be done stage by stage in co-operation with the Receiver to avoid dislocation. The first phase will be to take over certain selling functions which will be conducted by Rolls-Royce (1971) Limited, those concerned will be informed. Divisional operations should continue as at present. The Chairman of the Divisional Board is Mr H G Conway and the Managing Directors are:

Derby Engine Division	Mr G Fawn
Bristol Engine Division	Mr C J Luby
Small Engine Division	Mr J Perkins
Industrial and Marine Division	Mr R T Whitfield

The technical policy of the various divisions will be supervised by Dr S G Hooker as the Technical Director of Rolls-Royce (1971) Limited. Mr H E Trevan-Hawke and Mr D J Pepper continue respectively to be concerned with Finance as Director of Finance and Personnel matters as Director of Personnel.

A number of additional appointments will be announced later relating to Contract, Marketing and Production, to enable co-ordination and rationalisation of inter-divisional activity in these areas to be carried out.

Rolls-Royce and Associates Limited will operate as heretofore providing nuclear propulsion equipment for the Ministry of Defence. Dr D Mitchell continues as Managing Director of that company.

End
Chapel/Dickson"

An end and a new beginning. We were back in business again. To those of us at the coal face the whole thing seemed a complicated and unnecessary transaction.

One of the many consequences of the collapse which would have a far reaching effect on the fortunes of IMD was that the Ministry of Defence turned its back on the RB211 as a basis for a naval engine. This was later to give General Electric of America undisputed leadership in the naval market.

CHAPTER SEVENTEEN

Survival and success

From the point of view of those of us at Ansty who were involved, day by day, in the practicalities of keeping the business going, the three great trauma of the merger with Bristol, the takeover by Rolls-Royce and the Collapse, seemed events of less than crucial importance. We continued to invent, to design, to procure, to market and to sell the product. It was very much business as usual with revenue, year by year, continuing to rise. After all, Ansty had established itself as a major world supplier of industrial and marine gas turbines long before the sad event of February 1971 and we had an expectation of survival. And so it turned out. But achieving pre-eminence in this field had not been easy. The early attempts by Armstrong Siddeley in the 1950s to find a foothold in the industrial turbine market had not succeeded. Agreements with Brush in the UK and with Clark in the US to produce purpose-built industrial designs had not gone ahead.

It was the merger with Bristol and with it the availability of the Proteus and Olympus that gave Ansty the opportunity to move into high gear and create a strong and expanding business. The Power Division went ahead to become a major competitor in world markets and this position was reinforced by the Rolls-Royce takeover. The 60s and 70s were periods of unprecedented expansion and each market therefore merits its own story.

CHAPTER EIGHTEEN

Marine gas turbines

Attempts in Britain in the early years after World War II by the traditional steam turbine makers to produce satisfactory purpose-built marine gas turbines yielded no lasting success. But rapid progress in the evolution of the aero gas turbine had presented the naval world with the basis of a compact and reliable engine, at first at the lower end of the power range. The benefits of the high power to volume ratio and of reduced maintenance work load of the gas turbine had already been recognised by naval designers in the early 1940s for the propulsion of small craft used in coastal operations. The achievement of adequate range, however, presented a problem. The difficulty lay in the intrinsic efficiency characteristic of the simple cycle gas turbine. Fuel efficiency was a maximum at full load with progressive loss of efficiency at part load. For the propulsion of aircraft this was no real disadvantage since the power requirement to sustain flight at cruise speed was a high proportion of full power. In the case of a naval vessel, especially in the larger ships, power demand at cruise was a very much smaller proportion. For a frigate, the time average power demand was less than half the maximum. For patrol boats, however, range was rarely a decisive matter so fuel efficiency was less important.

When Rolls-Royce first proposed to the Admiralty that a gas turbine be specifically designed for naval use at power levels above those of patrol boats, it was not as an adaptation of an existing simple cycle aero engine. To meet the stringent specification for low fuel consumption at cruise, the Company designed an engine of considerable complexity and bulk involving the use of exhaust heat recuperation, separate low pressure (LP) and high pressure (HP) spools with intercooling and a free power turbine. By designing for a pressure ratio of 18 to 1, which by contemporary standards was exceptionally high and adopting this complex cycle, consumption at cruise was kept within the limits specified by the Admiralty. The design and development contract was awarded in 1946 and called for a maximum power of 6,000 hp. The overhaul interval was to be at least 1,000 hours, of which 300 were to be at full power and 700 at two-thirds power. Two of these engines went to sea in HMS Grey Goose in 1953. This ship, the first in the world to be powered solely by gas turbines, operated for over four years in UK coastal waters and in the Mediterranean. Despite its complexity and its early aero derived components, the RM60 engine achieved creditable reliability. Although the design showed promise, like the contemporary purpose-built engines derived from steam turbine practice, it was not to survive. By the time RM60 was showing its paces, the development of high speed diesels in Germany had led to the availability of turbocharged and intercooled designs which were more compact, more efficient and cheaper.

In 1954, a new requirement for Fast Patrol Boats had been identified by the navy, involving an increased maximum speed of 50 knots and a range of 400 miles. Despite the inclusion of high performance diesels in the competition and mainly because of the maximum speed required, it turned out that the Proteus, at a rating of 3,500 hp, was the only existing powerplant capable of meeting the specification. Although the early pioneering steps had been taken with RM60 at Derby and with Proteus and the first project studies of Olympus at Bristol, all the subsequent marine activity was centred on Ansty. Responsibility for this market had come to Ansty with the formation of Bristol Siddeley's Power Division in 1959. By this time the two Brave boats emerging from the Fast Patrol Boat requirement had been launched and Brave Borderer was undergoing sea trials. These were an outstanding success with Borderer exceeding 50 knots over the measured mile quite early in the trials and with a full armaments load. The marine Proteus had arrived and the adoption of the gas turbine had started which would lead to total acceptance of the aero derivative by the Royal Navy.

In 1959, Vosper, who had built the Braves, embarked on the design of a private venture fast patrol boat to be named Ferocity. It was smaller than the Braves and had only two Proteus instead of the three of its predecessors. The

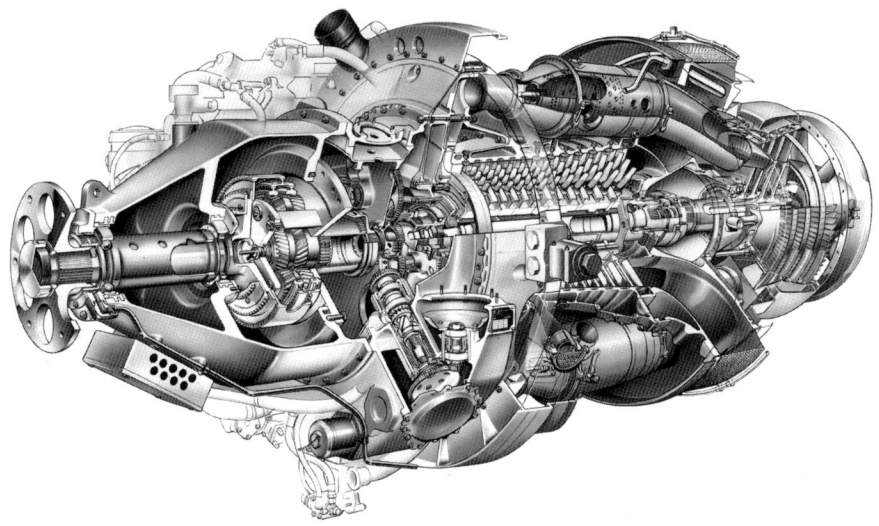

Marine Proteus

engines were, however, uprated from the 3,500 hp of the Braves to 4,250 hp. They were, in fact, engines removed from the Braves after they had completed 12 years of service. These same engines, now uprated, went on to work for another decade. During the 14 years following the commissioning of Borderer a total of 23 craft were built to similar hull designs by Vosper and were powered by Proteus. Though British interest in patrol boats was not to last, there were many other nations, notably on the Baltic, which would continue to use such vessels. Proteus engined boats saw service in the navies of Germany, Denmark, Greece, Libya, Malaysia and Brunei. In particular, Swedish interest in the Proteus was considerable. In all, some 274 Proteus had been sold by the end of the Seventies. It had been a great success.

The Royal Navy had, meanwhile, accumulated a great deal of service in escorts with the Metrovick G6 and the excellent operational qualities of the gas turbine had convinced the Navy by the early 1960s that all future escort vessels should include gas turbines at least as a part of their propulsion machinery. It was not, however, clear to the navy at this time whether future engines should be aero derivative or otherwise. A compressor failure in a G6 which necessitated a great deal of remedial work on board, did, however, highlight the advantages to be gained of repair by replacement. This capability was a feature of the aero derivative but there remained in the naval mind a lingering doubt as to whether an aero based engine would have adequate life. But in the decade 1953 to 1963, the lives of aero gas turbines in airline service had increased some eightfold and service lives in excess of 4,000 hours were being achieved. The possibility of replacing engines within a few hours offered much increased availability of the ship and the navy accepted that the balance of advantage lay with the aero derivative.

It seemed quite obvious to those in the business that the aero derivative was the right way forward because:

- Aero engine designs had incorporated the experience of more than a decade of continuous design effort by first class design organisations.
- The aero engine itself had a background of thousands of hours of service. The Olympus, for example, had been in RAF service for eight years when it was first ordered for the Royal Navy
- Manufacture in large numbers with comprehensive tooling made the aero engine a comparatively cheap engine in terms of cost per horsepower.
- It was compact and light.
- It was specially designed to start rapidly and to accept rapid changes in load.
- The aero engine was reliable and its reliability was well authenticated.

On the other hand, from the naval point of view, the aero derivative had certain features which required some development to fit it for this role:

- An aero engine spent most of its life at high altitude where pressure and density of the atmosphere was low. As a consequence aerodynamic excitation and thrust loads were lower than at sea level.
- It spent almost all its life in a very clean and corrosion free atmosphere.
- Aero engines were designed for shock loads significantly lower than those specified for naval operations.

Fortunately, only a comparatively minor programme of redesign and development was necessary to minimise the effect of these factors.

Bristol had begun to consider marine versions of the Olympus as early as 1957 and by March 1959 had issued preliminary performance data for a marine unit derived from Olympus 6. It was to have a continuous output of 18,500 hp with 22,400 hp available for short periods. The Bristol proposal, however, contained no serious consideration of the engineering of the power turbine. The design by Ansty of a purpose-built power turbine began in 1963 when the Ministry of Defence had indicated its choice of combined steam and gas turbine machinery in the Type 82 Guided Missile Destroyer with one Olympus and one steam turbine on each shaft. At this time the decision was made to choose a long life power turbine designed to stay in the hull for the entire life of the ship, provision being made to remove the power turbine rotor if and when necessary. The gas generator, comprising essentially the basic aero engine, would be removable for routine overhaul on shore. Following successful service experience with a prototype two-stage power turbine in an Olympus generating set, the marine version was to be of similar

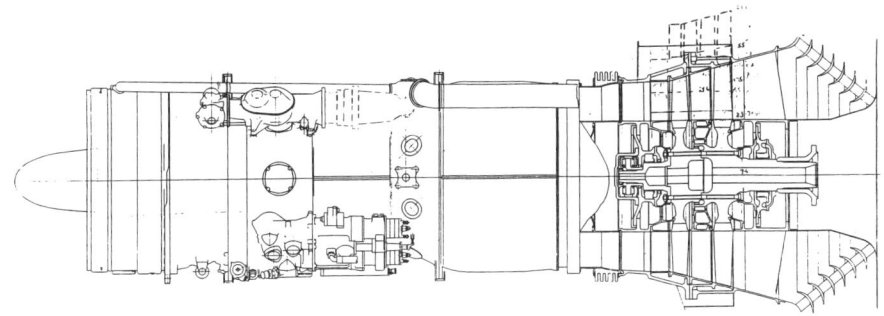

Project design of Marine Olympus from Bristol

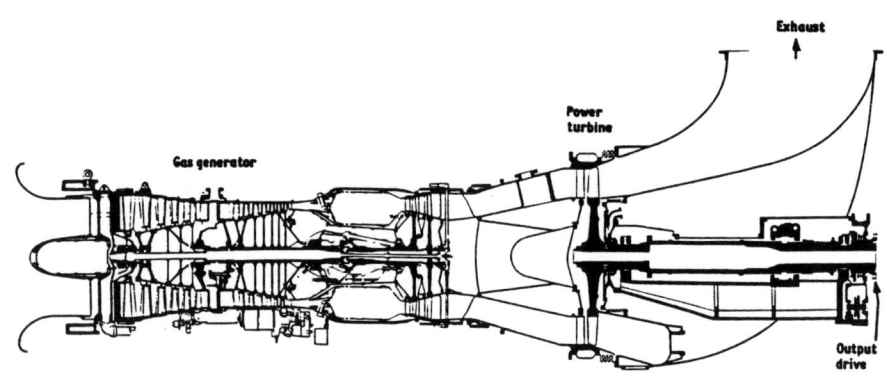

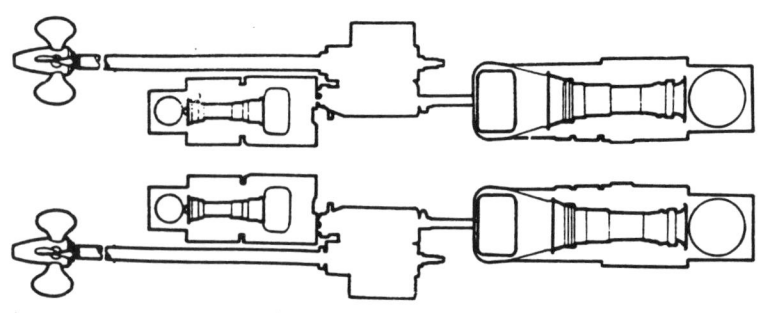

COGOG - BRITISH FRIGATES AND DESTROYERS
2 OLYMPUS 2 TYNES

Marine Olympus

style but with a single stage and speed raised from 3,000 to 5,600 rpm. The marine unit had an overall width of only eight feet thus permitting two engines to be installed side by side with adequate access within the beam of a frigate.

The first shore run of the new Olympus TM1A was carried out at Ansty in August 1966. By this time defence policy had cancelled further ships of Type 82 but the conversion of HMS Exmouth to all gas turbine propulsion with an Olympus TM1A/Proteus machinery fit had already started. Further defence policy changes also conditioned by budget restraints, now made it necessary to design the Type 42 which was a much smaller ship than the Type 82 but had, nevertheless, to fit the air defence system of the latter. There was therefore not enough space for both steam and gas machinery. Though there were good enough arguments for the choice of diesel machinery for cruise there were difficulties again with space. Thus the Olympus/Tyne fit came about and became a classic propulsion system fitted both to Type 42 and to the smaller Type 21. The common propulsion system for both ship types was based on a YARD Ltd design using the 21 mW Olympus TM3B and the 3MW Tyne RM1A with SMM (Stone Manganese Marine) controllable pitch propellers on each of the two shafts and HSDE (Hawker Siddeley Dynamics Engineering) machinery control. Both ship types were planned for the same timescale. In the event Type 21 (HMS Amazon) was the first to go to sea on 23 July 1974.

The Tyne had come to Ansty from Derby. It was very much better in terms of fuel efficiency than the Proteus. But it was an exceedingly costly engine reflecting its very sophisticated detail design. As an aero engine it was a propeller turbine in which both the low pressure compressor and the propeller were driven by the low pressure turbine. It did not, therefore, have the free power turbine necessary for marine propulsion. By a relatively small design change a free power turbine was engineered as an integral part of the engine. The more complex two-spool compressor of the Tyne as compared with the single spool of the Proteus reflected the advances which had taken place in the period which had elapsed between the design of the two. In particular, the Tyne had a design pressure ratio of 13.5 to 1 as compared with the 7 to 1 of the Proteus. Thus the Tyne had, at that time, an exceptionally high fuel efficiency, fitting its role as a cruise engine.

The Royal Navy's 1967 decision to opt for all gas turbine propulsion (both main and cruise engines) was a watershed in British naval engineering like the earlier change from sail to steam and that from coal to oil and from reciprocating engines to steam turbines. Within a decade this decision was to be put to the real test in the South Atlantic. Thirty-two ships of the Royal Navy were to be involved in hostilities often in appalling weather conditions and up to 8,000 miles from base. Of these ships, 19 were propelled solely by

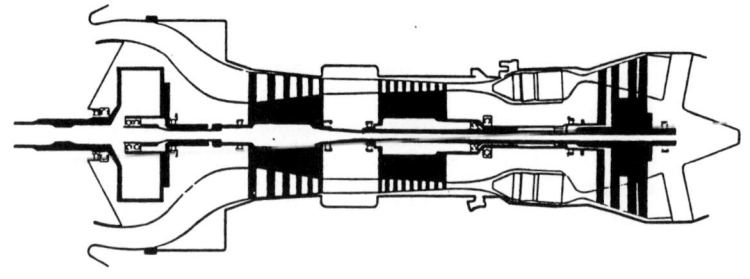

Aero

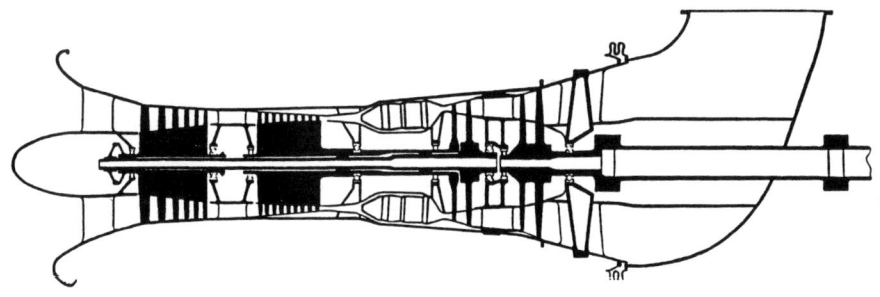

Marine

Conversion of Tyne aero engine

Ansty built gas turbines and of these vessels all but one had an Olympus/Tyne fit. The odd man out was the 19,500 tonne aircraft carrier HMS Invincible powered by four Olympus. Invincible broke all Naval records for continuous carrier operation by spending no less than 166 days at sea at a single stretch. From the fleet as a whole only two gas generator removals had to be made during the campaign. In the words of the Chief Naval Engineer Officer at the time, Admiral Horlick, "..........the overall performance was a real tribute to the designers, manufacturers, operators and maintainers".

HMS Invincible had two shafts, each driven by one or other of a pair of Olympus TM3B, each engine being rated at 28,000 hp (20mW) and connected via a reversing gearbox to a fixed pitch propeller. The decision to choose all gas turbine propulsion for Invincible was taken before Exmouth had gone to sea and thus involved a considerable act of faith. A review of the

HMS Invincible

performance of the ship at the end of its first year of operation concluded that the propulsion system had given an ideal match of redundancy and flexibility of operation and that good fuel economy had been achieved. In the year under review four engines had run together for only 5% of the time, whereas a single engine was operative for 35% of the time. Events had vindicated the propulsion system of this ship and especially the flexibility with which engines could be used.

In 1972 the Ministry of Defence issued a Statement of Requirements for a new engine intermediate in power between the Tyne and the Olympus. This emerged as the Marine Spey SM1A and became the British engine for the 1980s. At the outset the objective of the programme was to provide a machinery fit for four engines in a ship in COGAG (combined gas and gas) combination in which, as the Invincible arrangement, one, two, three or four engines could be used to propel the ship. Although the original idea was to develop a power unit primarily to be fitted in pairs on each shaft, the early applications in Type 23 were in a very different arrangement. In this frigate the SM1A was applied as an ahead only boost engine, cruise and manoeuvring being provided separately by diesel electric propulsion. This unusual combination was in response to a Naval Staff requirement for prolonged low speed operation and high top speed. Olympus and Tyne propulsion modules had been engineered to be fully capable of meeting the exacting conditions of naval warfare and to have a high probability of survival. The Spey programme incorporated all the know-how accruing from its predecessors but also brought the design up to date, introducing a good deal of later technology.

The gas generator was a derivative of the joint Rolls-Royce/Detroit Diesel Allison TF41 which was at the time of its choice the most powerful of the Spey family of aero engines. The Spey as a fan engine required a much greater change to its front end to convert it to function as a gas generator and a completely new low pressure compressor was designed. The marine gas generator was a two-spool axial flow unit with a design pressure ratio of 18 to 1, achieved by a five stage low pressure and an 11 stage high pressure compressor, each of which was driven by a two stage turbine. The combustion system had 10 separately removable flame tubes within a split annular casing. The maximum continuous rating was 12 3/4 mW (17,850 hp) (it had by now become fashionable at MOD to use the SI system of units) was achieved at a very modest level of exhaust temperature. This was very important in reducing the target presented to a heat seeking missile.

The power turbine was an entirely new two stage design which had a great deal of design office time spent on the achievement of high aerodynamic performance. In order to minimise tip clearances, the design was a departure

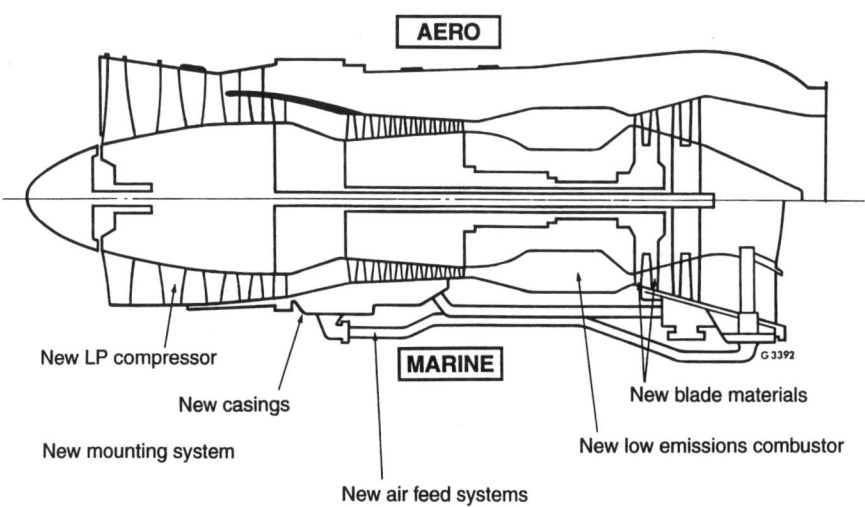

Conversion of Spey aero engine

from previous Ansty practice in having both an unsplit casing and a centrebody support structure.

Development of a low smoke combustion system turned out to be one of the major technical challenges of the programme. The aero Spey had been a very smoky engine and it was clear at the outset that drastic changes had to be made to meet the very stringent requirements of exhaust cleanliness laid down by the Ministry. The aero standard of combustor was abandoned and replaced by the Derby conceived Reflex Airspray Burner. This was their way of prevaporising the fuel air mixture and thus doing what the Siddeley Vaporiser had already achieved. Much development work was needed.

The Control System was integrated with the overall ship control and surveillance system, engine control itself having full authority over all the engine functions which were signalled by electronic machinery. This again was a departure from previous Ansty marine practice though experience with electronics had already been obtained on industrial units.

Considerable stress was laid in the programme on the combined objective of high reliability and maintainability of the whole propulsion module. This meant a massive effort in the application of failure mode and significance analysis. Each and every separate identifiable item in the entire system was scrutinised in terms of the way it might fail and of the probability of such

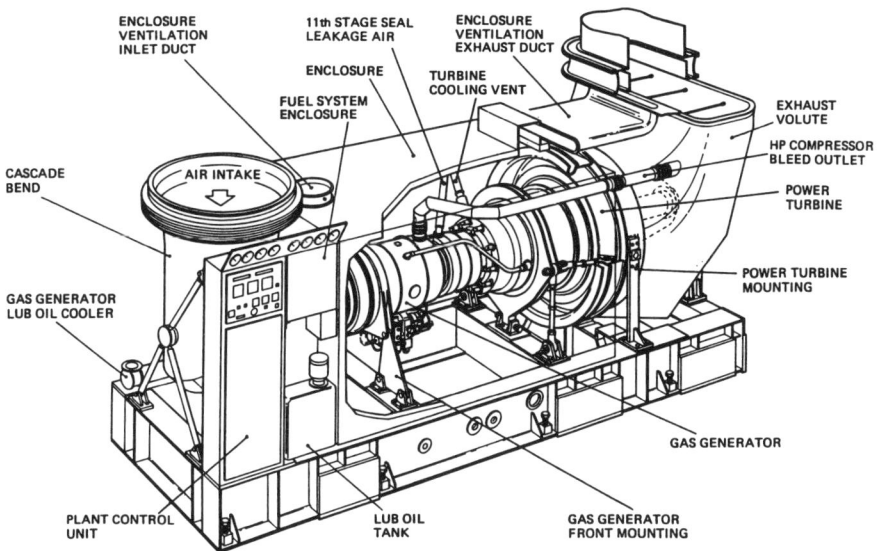

Spey propulsion module

failure. Critical effects were identified and the overall reliability of the whole propulsion plant was synthesised. It says much for the Reliability man, Gordon Healey, that throughout this mammoth enterprise he kept his cool and guided the work to its declared objective.

The management of the project as a whole was a combined effort by the Company and the Ministry. It included a considerable Maintenance Evaluation Programme led largely by the Ministry and a major source of inspiration at the design stage. The collaboration between the two parties over the programme as a whole led to a most satisfactory outcome though management difficulties did crop up from time to time.

CHAPTER NINETEEN

Hovercraft, a hope unfulfilled

Writing in the 1980s it was difficult to set in perspective the early enthusiasm engendered by hovercraft because the near extinction of the species seemed, in the light of hindsight, to be hardly surprising.

In 1953 when Christopher Cockerell submitted the idea of supporting a vehicle on a cushion of air it was hailed by the Press, and by at least a part of the engineering community, as an innovation of great importance. In the 1950s there was no shortage of money for new ideas and despite doubt about their viability, hovercraft were taken on. But the sceptics saw little advantage in a craft that was neither a ship nor an aeroplane and argued that this was an invention looking for a problem to solve. Such advantages as were claimed were seen as being of limited application. For example, as a military vehicle, a hovercraft could cross wide tracts of marshy land, a function denied to any other mode of transport at sea level. In many cases the marshes could, however, be bypassed by wheeled or tracked vehicles. As a ferry the hovercraft offered very much higher speed than displacement vessels, an advantage of great commercial importance but one which was very much dependent on fair weather.

Such considerations probably account for the slow response of the Ministry of Supply in sponsoring the new idea. The Ministry finally gave limited backing in 1957 to Saunders Roe, at first for a design study. Sponsorship of the programme was later taken over by the National Research and Development Council which set up hovercraft Development Limited the latter associating itself closely with Westland Aircraft and Vickers Armstrong. Each company built its own experimental vehicle, respectively the SRN1 and the VA1. SRN1, launched in 1959, was originally powered by an Alvis Leonides piston engine but this was later supplemented first by a Turbomeca Marbore, a jet of 800lb thrust and later by a Viper of 1,500lb thrust. SRN1 had a maximum speed of 68 kt with the Viper deployed for an all up weight of just over six tons.

Vickers Armstrong's original craft, the VA1, was a much lighter vessel weighing only 1.5 tons. It was powered by two piston engines, a 150 hp Gipsy Major for lift and a 133 hp Continental for propulsion.

The follow-on Westland design, the SRN2, launched in January 1962 was the first craft to be powered entirely by gas turbines. Both lift and propulsion were separately provided each by two Nimbus gas turbines of 815 hp. The Nimbus was an Anglicised version of the Turbomeca design, built at this time by Bristol Siddeley. This led to the involvement of Ansty as the support organisation. Shortly after SRN2 came the launch of the Vickers Armstrong VA3 powered by four Turbomeca Turmos of 360 hp each, also built under licence by Bristol Siddeley and in due course supported by Ansty.

In commercial application the economics of hovercraft were measured in operations over seaways in direct competition with ships and the margins of profit were marginal. Military applications, at least in the West, were limited to the testing of prototypes. The market for both applications never grew to a significant size and in these circumstances the funding of purpose-built engines could not be justified. The practice of adapting existing designs was to persist at least until the beginning of the 1980s. In 1962 the introduction of the long flexible skirt transformed the hovercraft from an interesting technical exercise into a practical means of transport. Encouraged by this technical advance, a substantial body of opinion came at this time to believe that it really had a significant place in the spectrum of commercial transport.

The launch of SRN5 in 1964 was a further step forward towards commercial viability in that a payload of two tons was demonstrated for an all-up weight of only 7.5 tons. SRN5 was powered by a single Gnome 1050, an engine of General Electric origin built under licence in the UK first by de Havilland and then taken over in the merger with Bristol Siddeley. The Gnome, which was also to power SRN6, was a high efficiency axial which, by the time of its introduction to hovercraft in the mid 1960s, had accumulated some 400 thousand hours in helicopters.

By far the most important of the British hovercraft was the SRN4, which entered service with British Rail on the Dover/Boulogne cross-channel route on 1 August 1968. It was still in cross-channel service in the 1990s though there were signs that there were difficulties in competition with conventional ferries and the Channel tunnel. It was still propelled by the trusty Proteus originally designed as an aero engine some four decades earlier. Although engines of better fuel economy had become available in the meantime, the volumes of business scarcely justified any change.

SRN4

At the outset, early success strengthened the case for the hovercraft especially the spectacular crossing of the English Channel by SRN1 in 1959 only two months after the start of sea trials. Indeed, the first two decades were marked by a series of technical successes and by steady improvements, notably in skirt design and in engine air filtration techniques. With the arrival of SRN5 adequate levels of payload were achieved and, as a more mature vehicle, this craft attracted the attention of the military. The Inter Services hovercraft Trials Unit, which had already built up some experience with SRN3, in 1965 took the more advanced SRN5 to Aden to carry out trials in the desert. The sand ingested by the engine turned out to be disastrous by causing very rapid erosion of compressor blading. The small blades of the Gnome suffered extreme damage, the first two engines lasting only six hours. Considerable success was, however, achieved by the follow-up development work to improve filtration.

When the Trials Unit took SRN5 to Libya some two years later the severity of the problem had been much reduced. Penetrating 200 miles into the Libyan desert the craft operated quite satisfactorily for 32 hours over sand and rock for the most part at a speed of 40 knots. The trials, albeit involving some patching of the skirt, were a success and subsequent engine inspection showed that it had at least another 300 hours of service life.

Travelling in its own cloud and emitting a level of noise typical of first generation turboprops, the hovercraft was not an ideal naval craft. There was no chance of approaching its target in anti submarine warfare with any degree of stealth and although the minimal disturbance caused under the surface of the sea made the hovercraft, at first sight, an attractive minesweeper, no advantage could be taken of the typical operating speed of a hovercraft because of the difficulties of minesweeping at such a speed. By the start of the 1980s hovercraft had made only a minimal penetration of the transport market and there appeared little chance of any significant improvement. Military applications by the Royal Navy seemed to have been abandoned.

Ansty's hope, though perhaps not its expectation, of engine sales in any meaningful quantity had not been realised. It seemed that the critics had been right.

CHAPTER TWENTY

Industrial gas turbines

In the early years of the 20th century the potential economic advantages of the gas turbine, which needed no boiler and was independent of water supply, were an alluring prospect. The first realisation of such a machine capable of producing useful power and operating on the familiar constant pressure cycle was achieved in 1939 when Brown Boveri installed the world's first gas turbine generating set at Neuenberg in Switzerland. Some 4mW of electrical power was produced from a simple cycle machine without heat exchanger. The design was based on steam turbine practice and at the relatively low temperatures and pressures which were then practicable, the fuel efficiency was poor. However, the low capital cost was an important advantage. Later the Swiss went on in 1945 to build a two-shaft machine with intercooling and reheat in a set producing 10mW.

In the United Kingdom installation of purpose-built gas turbines for the generation of electrical energy dates back to the late 1940s when two sets each of 15mW were commissioned in the North of England. They were designed for high annual utilisation and had complex cycles with heat exchange and reheat. Like the Swiss machines they had design features typical of steam turbine practice. Not surprisingly, the complexity of the design resulted in disappointing reliability and despite remedial measures over a long period, acceptable operation of these sets was not achieved and further development of this type in the UK was abandoned. In April 1954, addressing a Parliamentary committee on developments in industrial gas turbines, the Chief Scientist of the Ministry of Fuel and Power saw the prospects as very much limited as long as this prime mover depended on oil for its fuel. He strongly emphasised the importance of coal, a view that was later to be echoed at Ansty. The Chief Scientist predicted, however, that oil would remain the fuel par excellence for naval gas turbines.

The rapid post war development of the aero gas turbine, especially in terms of overhaul interval, encouraged the British electrical generating boards to be better disposed towards the aero derivative than they might otherwise have been, despite the use of distillate oil. This was certainly the case for peak lopping and standby sets for which the aero derivative was the only type capable of being put into service sufficiently rapidly to meet the urgent increase in the demand on the National Grid system. A factor persuading the makers to promote aero gas turbines for this purpose was the threat imposed in the 1950s by the government cut-back in its orders for military aero engines. But the start of application of the aero derivative in the

UK arose from the initiative taken by the Bristol Aero Works fending for themselves in this time of economic uncertainty. In 1956 the average working day consumption of electrical energy at the Bristol plant was some 300 thousand units costing almost half a million pounds sterling per annum. In particular, the consumption of electricity during daily periods of peak demand was very expensive and since the use of high power electrical plant employed in testing aero engines could not always be programmed to avoid the peaks, there appeared little prospect of controlling the expenditure. This became an increased cause for anxiety when, in 1957, the Sandys' White Paper made it clear that considerable reduction in production orders for defence would occur. A vigorous campaign was mounted at Bristol to save electricity in every conceivable way. After one year of effort, however, no significant reduction in cost had been achieved. Some 10mW of emergency diesel plant installed during the war was therefore put into service. A net saving in the first year of £90 thousand was achieved, even taking into account a heavy maintenance charge on the diesels. The practice of using the diesel sets primarily in a peak lopping role became established at the plant. In the following year a regenerative electric brake used in development tests on the prototype Marine Proteus was used to supplement the emergency diesels.

In 1959 the South Western Electricity Board, aware of this use of the Marine Proteus, asked Bristol to consider a modification of the Proteus as a generator for peak and emergency loads, particularly for isolated communities where existing connections with the National Grid were inadequate. These sets were expected to operate for periods totalling about 100 hours in a year to provide for peaks of demand. The requirements were straightforward as the engine was to be run at constant load and be governed by grid frequency. This mode of operation was greatly facilitated by the free power turbine of the Proteus. Such plant was first installed at Princetown, Devon, at an isolated site at an extremity of the Grid System and was the

Proteus at Princetown

Industrial Olympus power turbine motor

world's first remotely controlled gas turbine generating station. Demands were signalled to the HQ of the Electricity Board and the set would then be brought on load by dialling the station on the GPO telephone system.

Whilst a power of 3mW was suitable for temporary reinforcement of local electricity supplies and for standby duties, it could not make a significant contribution per unit to support the then 30,000mW capacity of the National Grid as a whole. This, and the success of the Proteus enterprise, encouraged the newly formed Power Division of Bristol Siddeley Engines at Ansty to investigate the idea of the application of aero derivative engines on a national scale. In 1959 a proposal was made to the Central Electricity Generating Board to consider the use of larger blocks of power burning diesel rather than kerosene in a derivative of the 200 Series Olympus as installed in the Vulcan bomber. This would be a gas generator to drive a purpose-designed free power turbine directly coupled to a 3,000 rpm alternator.

The 3,000 rpm power turbine design was undertaken at Ansty and had two stages. The Nimonic blades were supported from the discs in fir tree roots. The discs were connected by Hirth couplings and through bolts which were the means of attachment to the mainshaft. The shaft was supported as a cantilever by white metal bearings housed in a pedestal which also contained accessory drives. The stator casing was centralised relative to the rotor by attachments connected to a large cold ring, the latter being fixed to the baseplate of the power turbine. All parts of the power turbine in contact with hot gas were designed to expand freely and to accept rapid change in temperature without loss of concentricity.

The bearings were supplied with oil by the system supplying the alternator, thus ensuring that both the power turbine and the alternator shaft could be properly lubricated before starting to rotate. In later versions it was required to operate the alternator as a synchronous condenser for power

Olympus gas generator

factor improvement. For this purpose an automatic self-shifting clutch of SSS (synchro-self-shifting) design was interposed between the power turbine and the alternator. The power turbine was designed for a life typical of an alternator so that there would be no need to dismantle either during the life of the set. Maintenance of the gas generator was to be by replacement.

The prototype set with a Brush alternator was ordered in September 1960 by the CEGB as a 15/20mW turbo generator, the alternator generating at 11,000 volts and being rated at 20mW. The set was installed at Hams Hall near Birmingham in July 1962 and commissioned in September of that year at 15mW. Commercial duties started on 5 December and at the end of August 1963 the set was uprated to 17.5mW. Operations at Hams Hall in actual peaking operations, not unexpectedly, revealed early teething troubles both in the gas generator and in the automatic controls of the set. The causes of the engine problems were largely to be accounted for by the fact that the aero engine was developed to spend more than nine tenths of its operating hours at high altitude in a clean, low density atmosphere using kerosene, whereas peaking operations involved diesel fuel and much harsher conditions. Frequency of starts and rapid acceleration to full load were also more arduous than in aero service. In later years, when the CEGB's electrical distribution of power supplies via the National Grid had over 2,000mW of aero derivative plant on its system, it was calculated that the average running time per start was 41 minutes, the most frequent time being between 5 and 10 minutes. The latter would barely have covered taxiing time in an airline operation. At that time British Airways were operating with an average flying time of 115 minutes.

Shortly after the Olympus set was commissioned at Hams Hall a major blackout occurred in the south of England due to a sudden upsurge in demand which exceeded the capacity of the conventional steam sets and brought about a cascade of system trips. This event, together with an inability to build conventional steam plant sufficiently quickly to cope with the rapid increase in demand on the system, led the CEGB to provide each of the new 500mW steam sets with a standby gas turbine set arranged to provide the power to drive the steam set ancillaries in the event of drastic overload. Thus the cascade failure due to catastrophic drop in frequency on the system could be avoided.

Derby soon followed the pioneering steps taken at Ansty and Bristol by adapting the Avon for power generation. Derby, however, did not supply the whole set as a main contractor but supplied the Avon gas generator to English Electric and AEI who designed and built the power turbines and supplied the total set as main contractor. In the fullness of time, after Rolls-Royce had bought Bristol Siddeley, there was much debate about the pros and cons of the two ways of doing business but Ansty continued to main contract. The Bristol Siddeley sets followed closely the original Hams Hall design, the larger sets consisting of four such units in tandem, making a total of 70mW per set. The English Electric arrangement consisted of two Avon gas generators, each supplying gas to half the inlet annulus of a common power turbine, thus producing 28mW. A double ended arrangement of this was also supplied driving a single alternator of 56mW. This double configuration could be driven by either or both power turbines through self-shifting clutches. The AEI configuration was different again in having four Avons supplying gas to a single power turbine. This set was rated at 55mW.

Fifteen years after Hams Hall started, the CEGB were operating 2200mW of gas turbine plant on 29 sites in England and Wales. This represented about 4% of the Board's capacity connected to the grid. In addition, a further 1,400mW was to be installed by 1982. The record at December 1981 showed that Ansty had sold or had on order worldwide some 686 engines with a total rated power of 9,786mW. Over half these engines had been exported.

Although the aero derivative had made a late start compared with the

Model of 80MW Olympus set

purpose-built machine, it succeeded in making a significant penetration of the generating market. By 1969 it had taken a third of the total gas turbine sales in generation in megawatt terms. Taking stock of the position early in 1972 it was clear that generation would remain by far the largest gas turbine market and it was predicted that eventually the gas turbine could take a fifth of the total generation business in the Western World in a market growing at 7% per year. The Ansty share, however, was at that time less than 10% of the total of the generating market and there were disturbing signs that unless it could better meet the challenge of the purpose-built engine, this share might decline. An investigation of the costs of acquisition of a gas turbine generating set showed that only about half of the cost of a single Olympus set was accounted for by the gas turbine itself and that to achieve major reduction in cost per kW by the economies of scale of alternators and ancillaries it was necessary to build much larger sets. This could be achieved by multiple engines driving a single alternator, or better still, by designing the gas turbine for maximum unit power. For technical reasons, primarily related to blade stresses on the last power turbine stage, the theoretical maximum power output was just above 100mW and preliminary estimates indicated that such an engine driving a single alternator could bring down the cost per kilowatt to about 70% of that of the single Olympus set.

The story of the 223 at 100mW plus is a tale in itself. Design work on it went on for several years. During this time, Industrial and Marine Division had taken several long cool looks at the future of its power generation business. By 1974 the 'energy crisis' which had arisen from the Arab-Israeli war had become a worry. Although the long term objective of increasing the share of the electrical generation market was clearly expressed, there was some doubt as to the possible effect of this crisis. If coal and oil prices were to rise in step then the case for oil burning gas turbines for peak lopping would continue except that efficiency would now become more important and first cost less important. Thus the case for RB223 would be sustained in either single or combined cycle. It was recognised that in the long run coal burning regenerative gas turbines offered better economics than steam plant even for mid merit operation. The achievement of a larger share of the electrical generation market made it necessary to continue to make the best of the Olympus by raising turbine entry temperature, to introduce second generation gas generators of high efficiency, particularly the RB211, to continue with RB223 and to increase the R&D effort on coal gasification and regenerators.

The plan thus presented to the Chairman in January 1974 was adopted. The outcome, a decade later, saw successful development of a hotter Olympus(C) but as yet no exploitation of the RB211 for electrical peaking. Work continued for a few years on the RB223, a fairly detailed feasibility study being completed by the end of 1976. The report on the RB223 was quite unequivocal that despite what had now become a recession, the electrical generation market still offered the best opportunity for expansion of business at Ansty. The major features of the design had been determined and an adequate long term return on resources calculated. A very large adverse balance after five years was predicted with break-even after 11 years. But the prediction of sales of only 12 units a year did much to sap the confidence of the decision makers. Not long afterwards the project stopped.

In principle, however, the case for the large engine remained. By 1976 strong competitive pressures within the industry had resulted in price per kW being halved in real terms over the decade. The economics of scale had created a trend to larger sets and engines of higher power. Since RB223 had not survived, the next best big engine available to Ansty was the Olympus 593, the Concorde power plant. As the ultimate development of the Olympus family of aero engines it was the sort of engine we knew a great deal about. It was the world's largest aero core capable of 75% more power than the preceding industrial Olympus. Very importantly, it had been designed and developed to cruise at supersonic speed at pressure levels within the cycle much nearer to industrial conditions than was the case for any other aero derivative. The essential modifications to the aero engine involved relatively low risk.

A definitive design was prepared with a new three-stage power turbine. The objective was a single ended set of 48mW and a double ended set of 96mW. It seemed to be perfectly obvious that the Company should go ahead

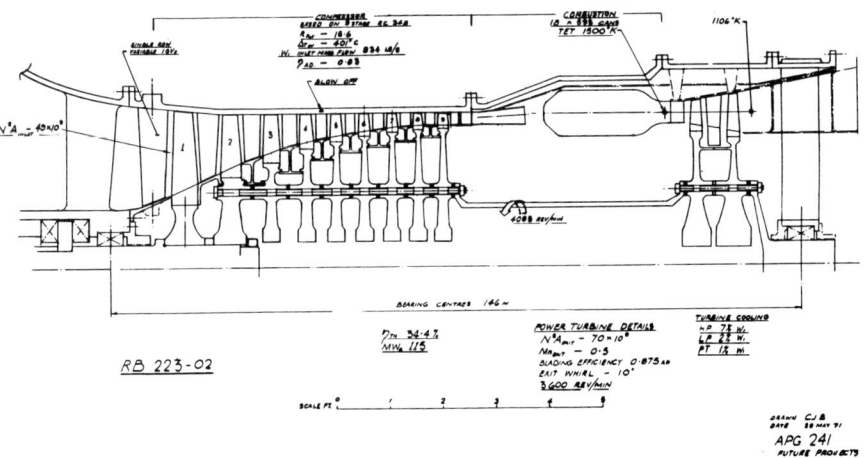

RB223 first model layout

MODIFICATIONS FOR INDUSTRIAL USE

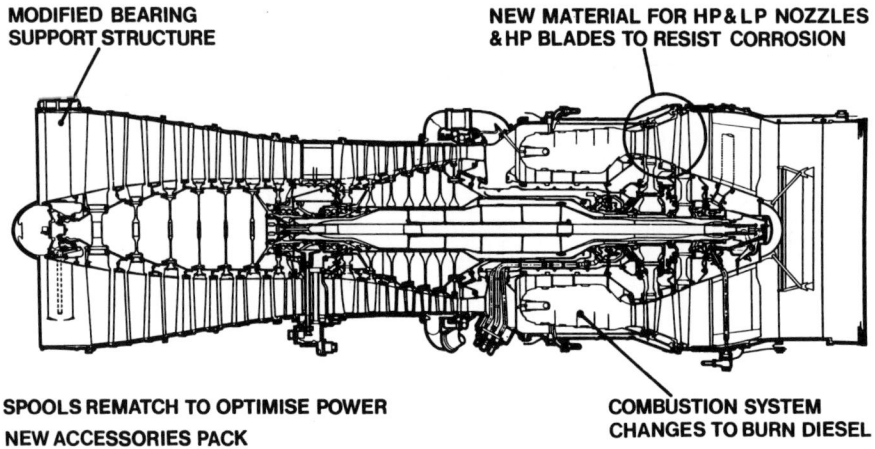

Conversion of Olympus 593

with this engine, which, by this time, had a 30 year pedigree. Its credentials were impeccable; calculated return on resources was acceptable though a major cost reduction plan for the gas generator was necessary. The programme started in 1974 with a target date for entry to market of 1981.

Not long after the Industrial 593 programme started, exceptional increases in material costs and a cutback in the aero production programme led to an unacceptable level of price quoted by Bristol for delivered gas generators.

Calculated returns on resources employed in the launch fell below the threshold of acceptability. To achieve a price competitive with published bids for sets from other manufacturers in 1975 meant a considerable reduction. Pending acceptance by HMG of the principle of applying differential overheads, the programme was frozen. In due course activity was resumed but this turned out to be only a temporary stay of execution for, in 1979 the Olympus 593, at a time of recession and in the face of irresistible price competition, notably from North American products, sank for good.

CHAPTER TWENTY-ONE

Gas and oil

The first successful adaptations of British aero gas turbines for purposes other than aviation began in the mid 1950s. By this time the earlier designs had become mature aero engines with longer overhaul intervals than those of the piston engines which they had replaced. The enthusiasm of their makers in proposing them as prime movers for marine or industrial applications was not at first reflected in the market place. It had to be done gradually and it was, therefore, as relatively small units for the propulsion of patrol boats or as support for a local extremity of an electrical supply network that they were first used. Not the least difficult of markets in terms of their resistance to the idea of this new prime mover, were the gas and oil businesses. The economics of pipelines were such that the capital cost of the line itself was dominant and thus the characteristics of the prime mover, except in terms of reliability, were of secondary importance. The traditional power plant were reciprocating engines and were the tried and the true. There had, however, already been some penetration of the market by heavyweight gas turbines of American origin.

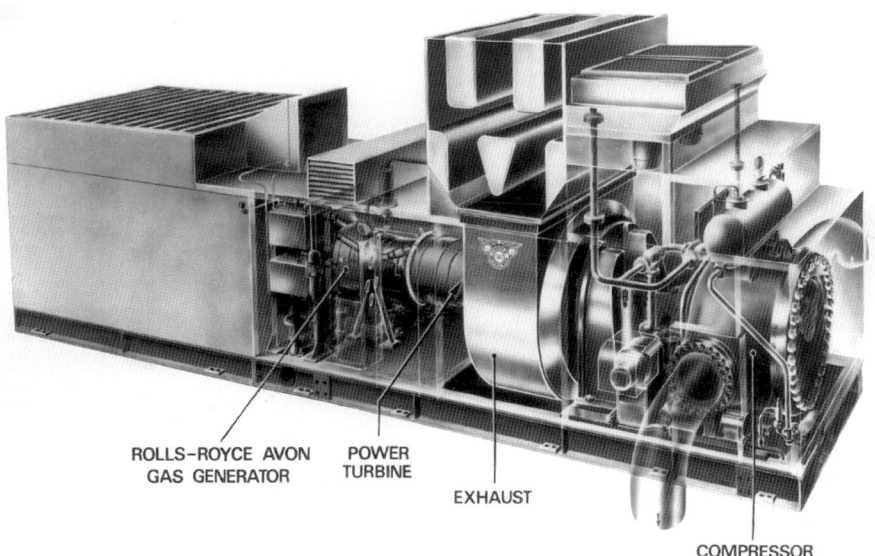

Cooper-Bessemer turbine/compressor unit

It was TransCanada PipeLines who broke the ice for the British aero industry by introducing the Avon into gas pumping service in the New World. The TCPL operation was of sufficient size to provide continuous base load operation for a large number of units. The system carried natural gas from the producing fields of Alberta to the industrial cities of the East. In 1964, ten compressor stations were installed using the Avon gas generator coupled to a Cooper Bessemer two-stage free power turbine which drove the pipeline gas compressor. The plant was required to operate for 90% of the hours of the year at remote sites where attendance for maintenance purposes would be only occasional. Remote operation had already been demonstrated elsewhere by the Proteus and the facility for rapid exchange of the Avon gas generator was of first importance. TCPL were aware that the high volume of aero engine production would guarantee availability of spares and they were impressed by the reliability record of the Avon as an aero engine, which had by this time achieved several million flying hours.

From this start the Avon prospered as a mechanical driver not only in pipeline operations but also in chemical process plant, for gas reinjection and oilfield pressurisation and for other uses. But despite its favourable operational characteristics, there were several design changes, albeit of a detail kind, which were necessary to achieve the full durability potential. When first installed in Canada in 1964 the average time between overhauls was approximately 1,500 hours. By 1971 the interval between overhauls had risen to an average of 21,000 hours and the fleet leader had clocked up 33,558 hours before removal for factory reconditioning.

Ansty became involved in the Avon following the takeover by Rolls-Royce in the Spring of 1967 when Avon people were transferred both from Derby and East Kilbride sites. Thenceforth all design and engineering activity was centred on Ansty, production of gas generators continuing to be the responsibility of East Kilbride. The record of the Avon as a driver was impressive. By the beginning of 1982, 571 Avons were on order or had been sold in this market. They had been exported to 33 countries, including the Soviet Union which had 56.

During 1972 discussions were held with TransCanada PipeLines about the possibility of improving the efficiency of their Avon pumping sets so that the volume of gas burned during transmission should be a minimum. It was envisaged that the rising cost of natural gas would fund the investment in higher efficiency. Candidates were a regenerative Avon and a Spey derivative. The difficulty with the regenerative Avon turned out, not unexpectedly, to be the design of a credible heat exchanger within the constraint imposed by the cost of the competing Spey derivative. The decision was taken to opt for a 16,000 horsepower version of the TF41 Spey. At this power level it was seen as appropriate both for refrigeration work on the 48 inch diameter line then coming along, and for pumping on the smaller diameter existing lines.

The case for funding the considerable launch costs of the industrial Spey thus derived depended on the belief in the early '70s that the replacement of existing Avons by the smaller and more efficient Spey would suffice to produce an adequate return on the investment. On this basis 20 sets of engine parts were ordered for the industrial engine. Some 20% lower on fuel consumption than the Avon, and of a size small enough to make handling easier, it was foreseen as having a substantially larger sales volume than the projected marine version. The decision to go ahead was taken with design release in September 1973 with the first gas generator run in September 1974, a very worthy effort bearing in mind the extensive changes needed. The first production engine, 001, was despatched from Ansty in mid 1976 and began trials with TCPL at the end of 1976. By the end of the 1970s it was clear that the predicted sales, at least in the early years, were not to be realised, though early teething troubles were relatively few.

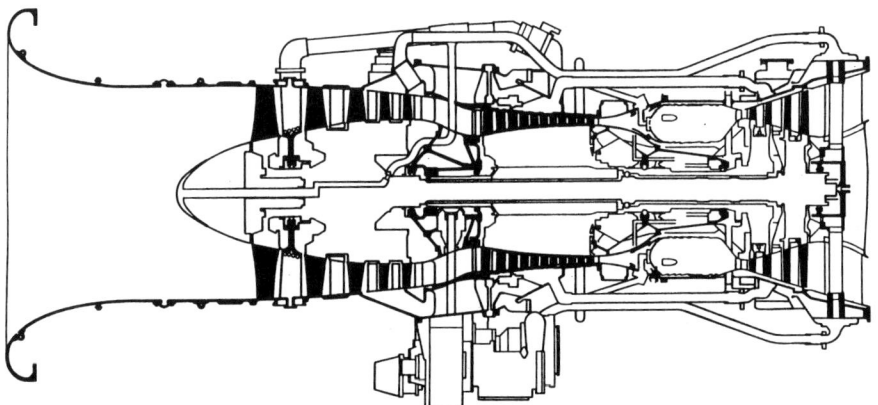

Industrial Spey gas generator

The development of pipeline systems had resulted in increased diameter of pipe and in greater distances between stations. Thus the trend was towards higher power and as the cost of gas in real terms was increasing, efficiency became more important. This naturally led to a proposal to adapt the RB211 for these purposes. Some preliminary design work had been done on a marine RB211 for the navy in 1969 but this work was abandoned when the Ministry of Defence turned its back on the engine following the crash of 1971, preferring to go for a marine version of the Spey instead. Work on the

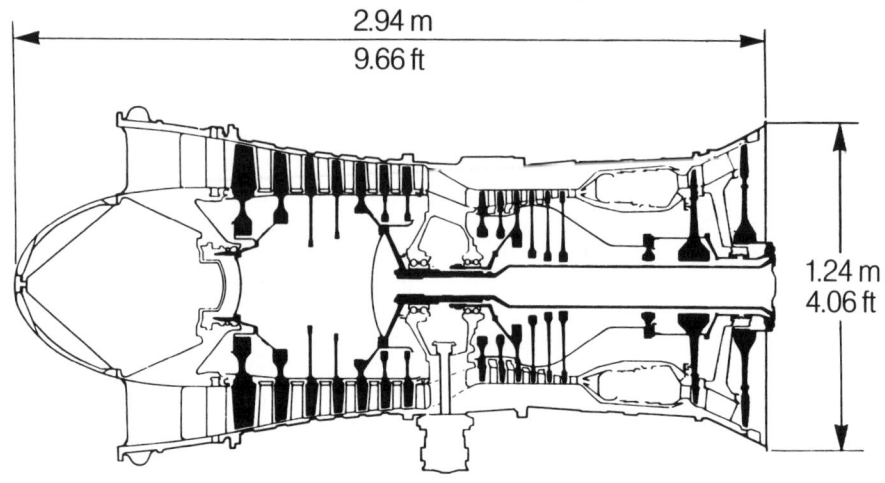

Industrial RB211 gas generator

Industrial RB211 however continued, the design of a gas burning version being started in 1976. The industrial engine was derived from the three-shaft aero engine by the removal of the fan, fan casing, accessory gearbox, fan turbine shaft, turbine and casing.

As the 1970s were drawing to a close, competition from the General Electric LM2500 was increasing and orders for Avon started to decline. RB211 and Spey sales were moving only slowly. Some means of assuring a better position in the market was clearly desirable. The then incumbent Managing Director, Humphrey Wood, proposed the idea of main contracting in gas and oil by setting up a joint venture with Cooper Energy Services, whereby Rolls-Royce would ally itself with a compressor maker to market complete pumping sets. Thus, in 1978, Cooper Rolls was formed with headquarters in Mount Vernon, Ohio. It certainly gave the impression of get up and go in the first two or three years of its operations.

CHAPTER TWENTY-TWO

New ideas of management

Rolls-Royce came to Ansty towards the end of the 60s and infused the organisation with a number of key people from Derby. More far reaching changes were later introduced by the reorganisation of the management structure. Rolls-Royce had arrived to find a traditional pyramid which was the legacy of the Armstrong Siddeley days. Those of us who had grown up in this system believed there was little in it to complain about, it was management by divine right, or so it seemed. It represented stability and we all knew exactly where we were. The high flyers slowly drifted upwards and finally came out at the top, to be followed by a fair proportion of middle management as it ascended the ladder. A few moved sideways. New arrivals almost always came in at the bottom unless they were Top People from elsewhere. Any other system seemed like anarchy. We did recognise one particular shortcoming of the pyramid. It frustrated the more impatient high flyers, who occasionally, but very rarely, quit. Most of the able people learned to cope with the pyramid and used it to their advantage.

The new system was introduced by Ray Whitfield, who had come to Ansty from Rolls-Royce & Associates in Derby to replace Bill Saxton as Managing Director. Bill Saxton had been the dour, forbidding boss who had come up through the pyramid. Ray Whitfield was a youthful physicist, bounding with new ideas and new attitudes. His approach was quite different. "My door is always open" he told middle management. He introduced several new classes of manager. Two of these, Market Managers and Product Managers, had authority to instruct functional departments. Reporting to the Board, the latter were to operate as mini-MDs. By definition, the Divisional Board continued to rule but a new type of middle manager had arrived on whom much responsibility rested and they were to be strongly motivated by the opportunities within their grasp.

Profit Plans were introduced and these were instantly recognisable as an improvement. The targets became visible and programmes of work made better sense. But perhaps the most effective change was government in which the MD would discuss the performance of the Division in open forum. It was in this business of communications that the new system was clearly an improvement.

We learned, for example, in 1970 that in the previous 12 months Ansty had made a profit of £439,000 as compared with £650,000 in the Profit Plan. The shortcoming was attributed to high overheads on Olympus, late deliveries of gas generators and a number of smaller problems. We found out

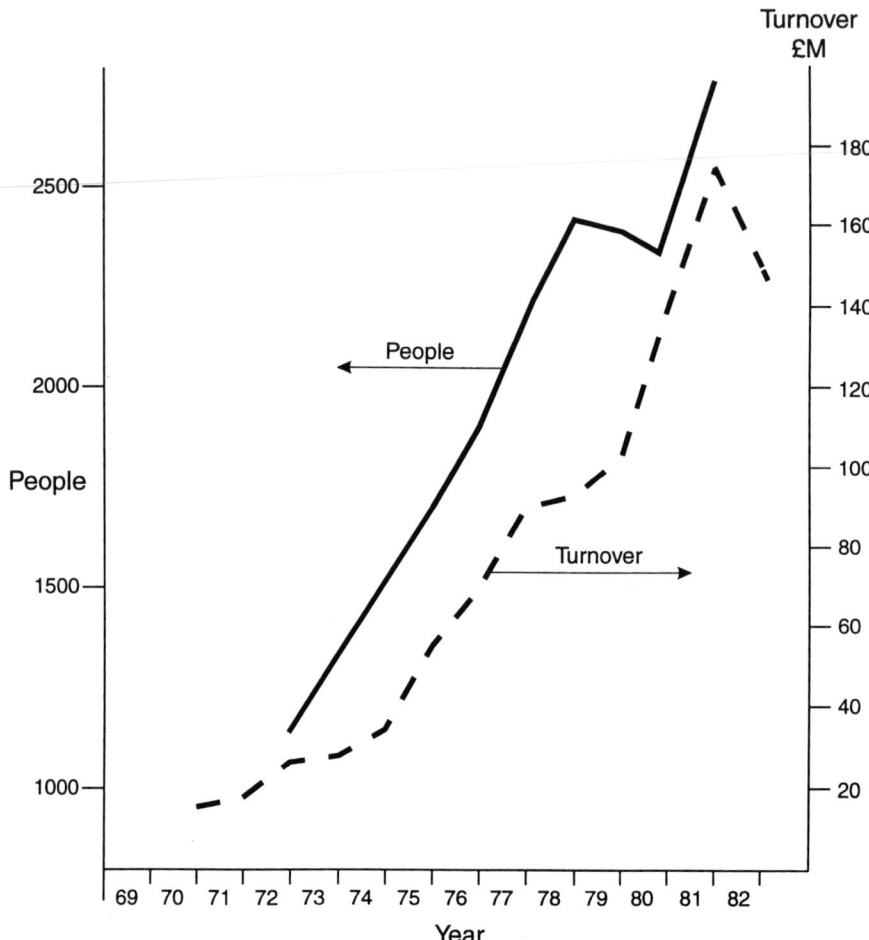

Growth of IMD – the years of expansion

how to do better and we passed the message along the line. We learned of the threat from excessive prices from our suppliers, not least from the Company's Aero Divisions. In terms of individual products the hovercraft market in 1969 was depressed and thus the Gnome had only a modest future unless things were to change. A dramatic increase in the price of the Proteus had forced a reduction in the predicted sales from a previous high of 45 to a level of 15 in the year. A project for the Dart had been identified in the US

ENGINEERS! JOIN THE INDUSTRIAL AND MARINE DIVISION

Since 1967, THE DIVISION
- Has doubled its size and trebled its turnover.
- Become Europe's major supplier of industrial and marine gas turbines.
- Successfully re-entered the main contracting field of gas turbine powered electricity generation.
- Is selling vigorously worldwide, backed by a strong home market.
- Has an order book of £100,000,000 plus.

OBJECTIVES
Further development of existing, proved engines.
Creation of a new engine generation.
Still further penetration of a world market demanding gas turbine power, particularly in the field of electricity generation.

IMMEDIATE NEEDS
ENGINEERS OF DIFFERENT SPECIALITIES:
STRESS ENGINEERS   DESIGNERS
PERFORMANCE ENGINEERS   (ELECTRICAL &
APPLICATION ENGINEERS   MECHANICAL)
DEVELOPMENT ENGINEERS   TECHNICAL AUTHORS

You are invited to come in for a private chat with a Senior Engineer, to see for yourself the working environment, and to ask any questions you like — of course, entirely without obligation. These informal discussions will take place on Thursday, 20 March, between 6 pm and 8 pm.
When it has been decided which particular Engineer you should see, prospective applicants will be seen in rotation. While waiting you can see a film about Rolls-Royce: a buffet will be provided.
Can't make the date? Then contact Mrs K. Brown, Personnel Officer, for an application form.

Rolls-Royce (1971) Limited, Industrial and Marine Division
P.O. Box 72, Ansty, Coventry, CV7 9JR. Telephone: Coventry 613211
At Exit 2 on M6 take A46 Leicester road through Ansty village. Turn right on to B4029.
Turn right under motorway bridge. Rolls Royce approximately ¼ mile on right.

Recruiting drive

but it had become far too expensive and the idea abandoned. The Tyne, however, was good news. The engineering programme to produce the free power turbine version for the navy had gone according to plan with a performance somewhat better than predicted and its naval sales potential seemed very good. Similarly prospects for the Marine Olympus were good. This first report on the state of the business had identified a marine version of the RB211 as being of first importance. (Unfortunately the crash of 1971 caused the navy to turn its back on this project). In 1970 it had already become clear that the power generation market was calling for blocks of higher power than were available from aero engine conversions. Albert Jubb proposed the monster Horizon engine as a purpose-built engine in the 100mW bracket. Though the Rocket business had made a significant contribution to Divisional profit, its future appeared bleak. No satellite was in orbit, Woomera had closed and Europa 3 would be fitted with someone else's engine.

Thus the newly formed Product Management saw the position and we were to go on with this clarity of view. The future seemed full of complication with many potential pitfalls but also full of challenge. It seemed at the time that the combined resources of the old Power Division and of Derby's industrial department were bound to succeed and indeed it turned out that we were at the start of an escalator that combined with a great deal of hard work would carry us forward to the status of a major industrial enterprise in its own right.

By the end of the 1965-75 decade, we had trebled the turnover of 1967 but despite exhortations to prevent it, the payroll had also started to climb. Turnover continued upwards as did the payroll at a remarkable rate at least up to the end of this story. These were the halcyon days with turnover increasing at an average rate of just under 18% per year. There was no indication, looking in retrospect at the curves, of any hitch due to either the crash of '71 or the oil crisis of '74.

The pressure of meeting the market demand fell largely on the engineers and campaigns were mounted to recruit new people. The 1975 advertisement in the local press bears witness to the perceived urgency of the situation.

Intense competition from the United States and the continuing difficulties of controlling cost made inroads in the later 1970s into profitability and reduced the freedom to pursue new products. By the 1980s the Division was producing an adequate margin only on the Marine Tyne, the Marine Olympus and the Avon. In each of the three main markets, sales revenue in real terms was showing reduced growth. The Division's hold on the power generation market was weakened. An industrial version of the Concorde engine, the Olympus 593, and the proposed large purpose-built RB223, had both been abandoned at the project stage. The Five Year Forecast showed that the new Olympus SK30, which was the basis of main contracting, whilst technically competitive, was somewhat expensive. In general, the market worldwide was depressed by large stocks of unsold GE Frame 5s. In the marine market the outlet in 1980 continued to be for warships. The early initiatives of the Royal Navy had made Rolls-Royce at one time the only supplier of aero derivative naval propulsion engines in the Western World. Since the later '60s, however, the international naval market had been penetrated increasingly by the Americans with the GE LM2500. By 1980 Ansty's future in this business was critically dependent on the Marine Spey. Success with this engine had already been achieved by its selection for the Royal Navy's projected Type 23 and for ships of the Japanese Maritime Defence Force. In the gas and oil market a high degree of customer satisfaction had been achieved with the Avon, which had become a leader in the aero derivative sector. By the end of the '70s, however, the customer was seeking prime movers of higher efficiency to match the increasing real value of gas and oil. The RB211 and the Spey were poised to take over from the Avon and to penetrate other sectors of the market where acceptance of the aero derivative had been slow. Predictions made in 1980 foresaw a capture of at least a third of the world gas and oil market, shared of course, with the Cooper Rolls organisation but it also recognised that new initiatives were needed to reduce cost and to ensure profitability of the new engines.

In the 1980 Five Year Forecast marine sales were expected to produce a more or less constant revenue in terms of actual cash and to produce an unchanged level of net contribution. Power Generation would produce a somewhat higher revenue and a better net contribution. Gas and Oil was predicted to improve in terms of both revenue and contribution. But overall, in real terms, there was little growth. The boom of the 70s had petered out.

Another new incumbent, Dr John Watkinson, introduced a further restructuring of management. The new Product Manager system had declined in importance and the new man had other ideas. The Division was to become more effective by forming Business Groups, each of which would be profit accountable. A Marine Business, a Power Generation Business, a Gas and Oil Business and a Product Support Business were therefore set up. The order book for 1981 was large and the new structure had to be at work as soon as possible. Morale, commitment and pace were the keynotes of the introductory address but we had to face the fact that we were overmanned by an estimated 15%.

By the end of 1982, when this view of Ansty ends, over 800 marine units had been sold, over 700 power generation units and nearly 700 gas and oil units. In aggregate these were capable of over 40 million horsepower.

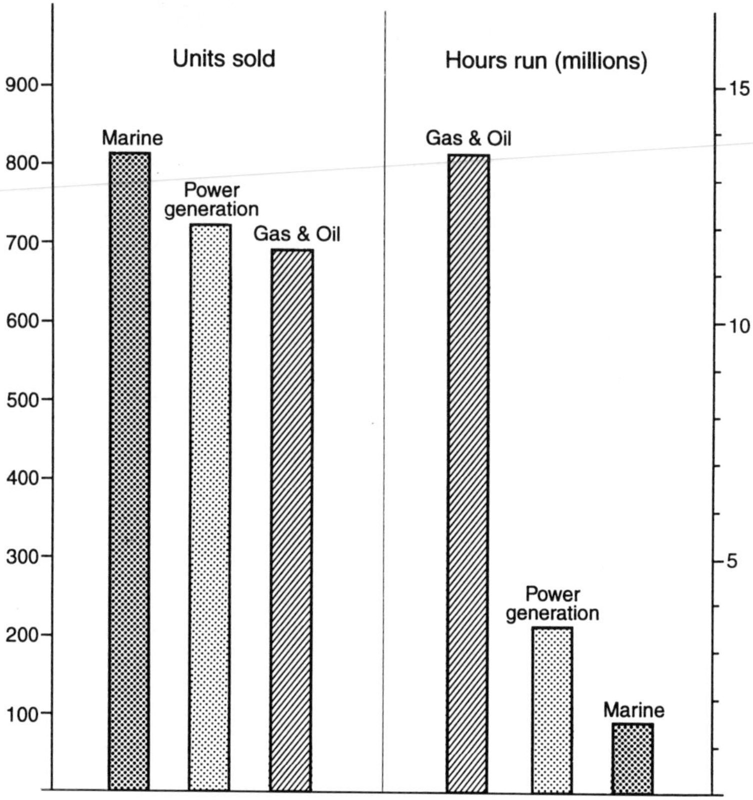

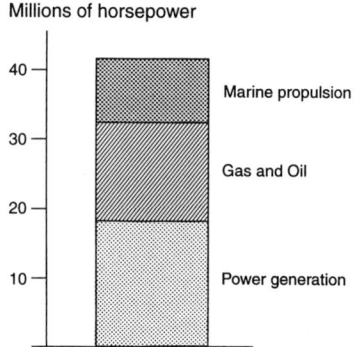

Achievements by the end of 1982

CHAPTER TWENTY-THREE

People

Though every one of the many thousands of people employed at Ansty during the years of this study had made a contribution, great or small, to the success of the business, the enterprise, like all major undertakings, was critically dependent on the quality of its leadership. Those in the more visible positions of authority are recorded.

Those who ran the show

The most outstanding personality in the Siddeley story as a whole was, of course, John Davenport Siddeley but there is no record of his presence at Ansty. He left the Company in 1936 having sold the Armstrong Siddeley Development Company to Hawker Aircraft. In this same year the flying training programme, operated by Air Service Training (AST) began on the aerodrome. Though linked with Armstrong Siddeley, AST operated independently and the flying school at Ansty came under an organisation with headquarters at Hamble. The man who ran the school was Flt Lt, later Wing Commander, R P P Pope DFC AFC, a man of great charm.

With the arrival of the Standard Motor Company, first to assemble Airspeed Oxfords and later de Havilland Mosquitos, the leading lights were Squadron Leader P V (Sam) Williams, the Chief Test Pilot who had been Chief Flying Instructor for AST, and Bill Wanley, who was in charge of the total Standard Motor Company operation.

In the mid 1940s while the site was still in the ownership of AST, Armstrong Siddeley began its first movements to Ansty. Starting with car test and despatch, there followed some work on the air starter motors for the ASX aero gas turbine and from July 1946 starting trials on the ASX itself. The pace of the transfer accelerated with the building of permanent test beds for Python and Mamba aero gas turbines which were occupied by November 1947. By the end of 1949 some ten major test facilities had been built. During these first years there was only a small establishment of personnel on the site and this remained the case until the occupation of the new Engineering Centre in 1957-58. Administration of the development staff, many of whom travelled out day by day, was centred on Parkside under the ultimate leadership of H T (Tom) Chapman, Managing Director, W F (Bill) Saxton, Chief Engineer and W H (Pat) Lindsey, Deputy Chief Engineer. This triumvirate was to run Armstrong Siddeley until the merger with Bristol.

H T Chapman had joined Armstrong Siddeley in 1926 after leaving

Armstrong Whitworth in Newcastle-upon-Tyne where he had been involved on the design side. Starting at ASM in the Aero Engine Drawing Office he was concerned with the design of the early air cooled radials, notably the Mongoose. Transferring later to the manufacturing side of the business he was to rise to the position of Managing Director. He ran the Company with a firm hand, though not without charm.

W F Saxton, a man of large physique, had been a rugby player of considerable merit and was a natural leader. With a strong will and a somewhat forbidding appearance, he had a sense of humour, albeit occasionally at someone else's expense. Joining the Company in 1924 he was involved on the manufacturing side and in 1941 became Quality Manager. It was in this job that he earned a place during the War in the Honours List. By 1945 he had become Chief Engineer and this led to a dramatic new competence in Design and Development at Armstrong Siddeley. In 1950 he became a director and in 1953 Director and General Manager. He became Deputy Managing Director in 1957 and following the merger with Bristol, became Production Director of Bristol Siddeley. He was appointed Managing Director of the Power Division in 1965 and, with the arrival of Rolls-Royce, this was translated to the office of Managing Director of the newly formed Industrial and Marine Division.

W H Lindsey joined ASM in 1933, having graduated from Cambridge with a First in the Mechanical Sciences Tripos. An intellectual of great clarity of vision, he masterminded the engineering activity both at Parkside and at Ansty for almost 30 years. Working in relative obscurity in the Aero Engine Research Department, he was involved early in his career, with the development of the two-speed supercharger for the Tiger VIII. In 1942 ASM was awarded a Ministry contract to develop the ASX turbojet. He was now in charge of the Research Department and had set foot on a path which was to take him to the seat of the Director of Engineering in the Industrial and Marine Division. A somewhat distant person, he was however, able to complement the opposite character of W F Saxton and this partnership was recognised by the award in 1958 by the Royal Aeronautical Society jointly to them of the Silver Medal for Aeronautics, recognising their work in aero engineering. The ASX had been designed in aerodynamics and layout at Farnborough and Armstrong Siddeley carried out the mechanical design and development, but the Mamba had its origins at Parkside and Lindsey took a major part in its creation. In 1949 the Royal Aeronautical Society awarded him the Herbert Ackroyd Stuart Memorial Prize for his classic paper "The Development of the Armstrong Siddeley Mamba Engine". In 1945 he became Deputy Chief Engineer reporting to W F Saxton. By this time the turbine programme had reached the stage of flying the ASX in a Lancaster flying test bed. In 1956 there were five different types of engine in production for the RAF and the Navy, WHL having been technically responsible for all of these. Not least of his achievements was the bringing together of a group of brilliant young engineers and organising them into a first class team. These were the men who would form the technical backbone of the Power Division at Ansty and of the later Industrial and Marine Division. When Rolls-Royce came to Ansty and set up IMD, W H Lindsey became the Director of Engineering.

S (Sidney) Allen was one of the stars in the Lindsey firmament and came to Armstrong Siddeley in 1934 after leaving Petters of Yeovil. Sidney Allen was a brilliantly resourceful engineer whose success owed much more to imagination than to academic skill. As the inventor of the Armstrong Siddeley Vaporiser, he had found a place in the history of aero engine technology. He began his career as a junior designer in the Research Department at Parkside and in due course took over the development work on single cylinder research engines. This led to his leadership of the development of gas turbine combustion systems. He set up the Combustion Department and as Chief Combustion Engineer reporting to W H Lindsey, was responsible for the development of all combustion and reheat systems. Always at his best when involved with smoke and flames, he took naturally to the business of Rocket Motors and relinquishing his leadership of the Combustion Department which he handed over to M A (Morris) Stokes when he became Chief Rocket Engineer. In 1958 he was appointed Chief Engineer of ASM and on the formation of the Power Division was appointed its Chief Engineer responsible for Rockets, Industrial and Marine Gas Turbines, Diesels and SRM Transmissions. After the formation of IMD Sidney Allen became its Chief Designer.

B H (Brian) Slatter joined Armstrong Siddeley in 1940 after graduating at Manchester University. Possessed of a first class analytical mind, Brian was the man whose engineering opinion no one could afford to ignore. His work on turbine engines began in 1941 and coming under the wing of W H Lindsey in 1942 he was seconded to Farnborough. He returned to Parkside in 1943 to join in the development of the ASX and its conversion to the Python. In that year he carried out the flight evaluation of the ASX in the Lancaster flying test bed, as Flight Test Observer. Setting up the Flight Department at Parkside and at Bitteswell he was responsible for the performance work on all Armstrong Siddeley turbine engines. In 1958 he became Deputy Chief Engineer (Research and Development). In 1963 he was made Chief Engineer (Turbines) retaining this position on the formation of the Industrial and Marine Division. In 1973 he was appointed Director and Chief Engineer of IMD. Through the four decades of his career Brian exercised remarkable skill in analysing situations and in separating the technical wheat from the chaff to great effect. His contribution to the development of the aero derivative marine gas turbine was recognised by the invitation of the Institute of Marine Engineers to read the 19th Parsons Memorial Lecture. His work in the industrial and marine business, first of Bristol Siddeley and then Rolls-Royce, was of decisive importance in the creation of a significant industrial enterprise.

J (Johnny) Marlow began his career after graduating at Leeds University with the Engine Division of British Aircraft Corporation transferring to Alvis in 1937 and joining Armstrong Siddeley in 1940. Like the other bright young engineers at Armstrong Siddeley, he joined the Research Department and in 1943 was at work with Brian Slatter on the ASX. In due course he took charge of engine development and by 1958 he was Deputy Chief Engineer (Development) reporting to Sidney Allen. A year later this bluff, good humoured Yorkshireman had left Ansty to join the team at Bristol where he was to continue a distinguished career in engine development, notably on the Viper.

A (Bert) Thomas was the key figure on the design side. Starting his career at Derby as an office boy in 1918 Bert came to Parkside as a Senior Draughtsman in 1928. His first major job with Armstrong Siddeley was the design of the propeller reduction gear of the Leopard. After a relatively brief spell from 1934 to 1936 with Cierva and with Wolseley he returned to Parkside and was much involved in the design of the Cheetah. In 1947 he was appointed Deputy Chief Engineer and Chief Designer reporting to W H Lindsey. In 1949 he was awarded an MBE for his services in the aero engine field.

Responsibility for Commercial and Marketing as a combined activity first became clear with the appointment of F T Blakey as Special Director and Business Manager of the Power Division in 1959. F T (Frank) Blakey was a relatively late arrival at Armstrong Siddeley. His previous career had been in the motor industry. He had held a series of appointments with the Nuffield Group before becoming Chief Cost Accountant with the Austin Motor Company in 1949. He joined ASM in 1953 as Secretary.

In the year following the establishment of ASM in the new Centre at Ansty, the merger with Bristol came into effect, W F Saxton went to Bristol as Production Director of Bristol Siddeley and W H Lindsey also became a Director on the Bristol Siddeley Board, though staying at Ansty. A number of the Armstrong Siddeley aero engineering team transferred to Bristol and contributed significantly to the strength of the new Bristol Siddeley aero engineering function.

Frank Blakey now reported to Basil Davidson, the Business Director at Bristol. The Power Division management was little more than a modification of its Armstrong Siddeley predecessor, reflecting the decision to concentrate the aero engine work at Bristol. Ansty gained a new manager in the person of

C E M Preston. Cdr C E M (Chris) Preston had served in the Royal Navy from 1936 to 1958, mainly in frigates and destroyers. In 1953 he was appointed Trials Officer, Coastal Forces, and was associated for the next three years with the design and development of gas turbine machinery for Fast Patrol Boats. In 1958 he joined Bristol Aero Engines in charge of Marine Gas Turbine Sales. On the formation of Bristol Siddeley Engines, he was appointed Gas Turbine Sales Manager and became General Sales Manager in 1962. Chris Preston was appointed Director of Marketing of IMD in 1974 and became Director of Marine Marketing in 1977. Chris was an extrovert with memorable characteristics and was one of the 'personalities' on the Ansty scene.

By the mid 70s the Industrial and Marine Division was in full swing. Some idea of the expansion of the business can be gained by comparing the chart of the Engineering Organisation for 1976 with that of the engineering team that started Ansty off in 1958. There were now almost twice as many names. The overall Divisional Organisation for the following year reflects the increasing emphasis on Marketing, Product Support and Product Management. The Division now reporting to J H A (Humphrey) Wood had no less than eight Directors but under the leadership of his successor Ansty lost the status of a self-standing Division and had become Rolls-Royce Ansty.

Up to the end of this history Ansty's first Managing Director, W F Saxton, had been followed by five successors, namely:

R T (Ray) Whitfield
R H (Ralph) Robins (later Sir Ralph)
J H A (Humphrey) Wood
J F (John) Watkinson
P F (Peter) Macfarlane

R T Whitfield graduated in Physics at Durham. He served in the Royal Naval Scientific Service and then worked with the Vickers Armstrong team on the Nuclear Submarine Project at Harwell. He jointed Rolls-Royce and Associates in 1960 as Chief Physicist and became Managing Director and Chief Executive of RR&A in 1967. In 1968 he succeeded W F Saxton as Managing Director of IMD. There could scarcely have been a greater contrast between the two. Ray Whitfield brought new ideas of management to replace the paternalistic style of his predecessor. We now had open government with an emphasis on communications. R T Whitfield set the Industrial and Marine Division on the course to take advantage of the boom of the 70s.

He was succeeded in May 1973 by R H Robins. A graduate of London University, Ralph Robins began his career with Rolls-Royce in 1955 as a graduate apprentice. In 1962 he was Project Accessory Engineer – Conway

Ray Whitfield and the Naval Overseer 'top out' No 66 test house

and in 1965 he became Deputy Development Engineer Conway 42 and 43 and Senior Staff Officer Spey in 1966. In 1970 he was appointed Assistant General Manager Marketing and in 1972 moved to the US to become Executive Vice President Rolls-Royce Aero Engines Inc. Ralph Robins took up the baton from Ray Whitfield and accelerated forward. During his leadership IMD continued to sell vigorously worldwide, backed by a strong home market. IMD became Europe's major supplier of industrial and marine gas turbines. For the first time the order book exceeded £100 million and by 1973 the Division had doubled its size and trebled its turnover since the beginning of IMD in 1969.

The next Managing Director was J H A Wood who had graduated in Mechanical Science at Cambridge. He joined the de Havilland Aircraft Company in 1956 as an aerodynamicist. Thereafter when the Company had become part of the Hawker Siddeley Group he moved to the sales side becoming Commercial Manager in 1964. In 1966 he was appointed Executive Director Commercial for the Manchester Division and in 1968 appointed to the Hawker Siddeley Board as Director and General Manager Manchester. Humphrey Wood came to Ansty in September 1976. He arrived at a time when the backlash of foreign competition, notably from the United

States, had begun to make itself felt. Profitability had begun to decline and to protect its position in the markets, the Division had committed itself to substantial investment in new products. Following the example of main marketing as a method of securing a position in the market, Humphrey Wood introduced a new company, Cooper Rolls, to assure a place in gas and oil.

Next Dr J F Watkinson was on the scene, this time as Company Director Industrial and Marine, arriving towards the end of 1979. Having graduated in metallurgy at Sheffield he had held a number of appointments in that field. In 1976 he had become Divisional Managing Director of the Plessey Group. By the time he joined Rolls-Royce at Ansty only a minority of the Division's products were enjoying adequate margins. The current Five Year Plan showed no growth in any of the three market sectors. He created Business Groups as accountable profit centres and removed a good deal of slack from the cash flow.

The View of Ansty ends with 1982. In September of that year Peter Macfarlane arrived to succeed Dr Watkinson as Director Industrial and Marine. Trained as an accountant he had spent several years in Nigeria for Coopers and Lybrand. After a number of subsequent appointments in Europe and the Middle East he returned to the UK to serve with British Leyland, becoming Assistant Treasurer of that company. He joined Rolls-Royce in 1979 as Group Treasurer.

Other notable top people

Until the time of Dr Watkinson, IMD had been administered by a Divisional Board, comprising representatives of each major function. In particular, there were three who were really memorable, namely, H R (Bert) Beattie – Production and Services, K O (Ken) Crooks – Product Support and J (Jack) Dent – Finance.

H R Beattie had graduated in Engineering at Bristol and joined Avro in 1959. In 1967 he became Commercial Manager of the Manchester Division of Hawker Siddeley Aviation and in 1970 Commercial Director. He joined IMD in 1977 as Director of Production and Services and was appointed General Manager and Deputy to the Managing Director in 1979. Production, never a straightforward business at Ansty, not least because of the difficulties of controlling supply from the Aero Divisions, had become his responsibility and he sorted it out. During the interregnum between Humphrey Wood and John Watkinson he ran Ansty.

K O Crooks became Chief Stress Engineer at Derby in 1958. In 1962 he joined Rolls-Royce Canada as Vice President Engineering and later became Executive Vice President Rolls-Royce Aero Engines Inc in New York. In 1970 he moved to Ansty as Production and Service Director IMD. Both a witty man and a forceful man, Ken was never given to mincing his words and was notable for the straightforward way in which he conducted discussions with major customers, saying his piece without fear or favour. As the workload on the Service Department increased he took over this function, together with Technical Publications, to form a new Product Support department.

J Dent came from a Systems Analysis background at Derby and took over control of Finance at Industrial and Marine Division. It was Jack who, as Finance Director, skilfully husbanded the financial resources during the expansion of the 70s. Between the departure of Ralph Robins to Buckingham Gate and the arrival of Humphrey Wood, Jack held the fort at Ansty. He had that Kiplingesque ability to walk with Kings without losing the common touch.

Survivors from Armstrong Siddeley

There were a number of senior people in the Armstrong Siddeley days who were still in positions of authority as the 70s came to an end. Six of these were identified on the Armstrong Siddeley Technical Organisation Chart for 1958 and were: B H Slatter, T G Daish, M A Stokes, H Saville, A W Broomfield and A W T Mottram.

T G (Geoff) Daish, who had graduated from Cambridge and had been one of the Whittle team at Lutterworth, came to Armstrong Siddeley in 1946 when the Power Jets team was disbanded. He joined the newly formed Flight Section under Brian Slatter. Continuing the specialisation he had developed with Power Jets, he became Ansty's unquestioned authority on performance. After leading the Development team on Marine and Industrial gas turbines in the Power Division he later became the Chief Technical Services Engineer of IMD. A stickler for seeing the job through with meticulous attention to detail, Geoff also acquired a wide reputation for his poetry, recommended to those seeking more of an inside view of his life and times.

M A (Morris) Stokes had trained as an electrical engineer and started a three year apprenticeship with ASM in 1937. Having served his time, he became a member of the Research Department at Parkside working with Sidney Allen on single cylinder research. When Armstrong Siddeley took up gas turbine engines in 1943, he continued to support Sidney Allen in the new business of turbine combustion systems. In 1954, Morris became Chief Combustion Engineer and after the formation of the Power Division he took over responsibility for the Maybach Diesel and the SRM Hydromechanical Transmission as Chief Engineer (Diesel and Transmissions). Latterly appointed as one of Ray Whitfield's Product Managers, he handled the Marine Spey in its early years. Morris achieved a considerable extramural reputation for his skill as a golfer.

H (Harold) Saville graduated in Mechanical Engineering at Manchester University, joining Armstrong Siddeley in 1940. In 1942 he joined the Royal Navy and at the end of the War went to Metropolitan Vickers at Trafford Park. After Metrovick abandoned their work on gas turbines he returned to ASM. As a widely recognised expert in the technology of control systems, Harold was responsible both in the Power Division and IMD for the hydromechanical and electronic systems of electrical generating sets, gas and oil drivers and for the propulsion controls of naval ships.

A W (Arthur) Broomfield had graduated at Southampton and joined Armstrong Siddeley in 1948. His assignment was in Project R, the embryo Rocket Department, at that time a section of the Combustion Department. He became the one and only Development Engineer in the early days of the Rocket programme at Ansty becoming later Engineer-in-Charge Rocket Engines. In 1972 he was awarded the MBE for his services to the development of this technology. By 1972 when the rocket business at Ansty came to an untimely end, Arthur had become Engineering Manager. He was the last to leave the rocket activity and had the sorry task of shutting the door. Thereafter he joined the Gas Turbine Development Department as Senior Development Engineer.

Another survivor of the ASM days who also became a casualty of the unfortunate decision to abandon rocket work in the UK was A W T (Tony) Mottram who had qualified at Manchester. Joining Armstrong Siddeley in 1948 he became one of the first members of Project R. He became responsible for Rocket Research before the demise of ASM and maintained this function until the end of the rocket business at Ansty in 1972. Heading the Advanced Projects Group of the Power Division until the formation of IMD, he was later to nurse the ill-fated RB223 Industrial engine during its short post project stage.

There were many others who had started at Parkside and were still in positions of authority at Ansty as the 70s drew to a close. Three quite prominent such survivors were D C (Don) Austin, H J (Jack) Prince and N R (Norman) Jones.

Don Austin joined Armstrong Siddeley after serving in Military Intelligence. After the formation of the Power Division he became assistant to Frank Blakey and later took over the Contracts activity of the Rocket Department. Having developed an exceptional skill in the art of negotiation with the British Government he took over the whole business of contractual work associated with the booming naval business of the 70s.

Jack Prince had serviced an apprenticeship with Armstrong Siddeley. After service during the war with the RAF he returned to Parkside to work on Fuel Systems in the Gas Turbine Experimental Department reporting to the unforgettable Jimmy Jagger. In 1959, after the formation of the Power Division at Ansty, he was appointed Sales Manager Nuclear Reactor Components. Thereafter he was busy selling Proteus and Olympus to the electrical generation market, then with sales to the oil and gas industry, where his name became world renowned. In 1976 he was appointed Executive, Industrial Marketing. Jack was a character whose robust sense of humour was well exercised.

Norman Jones joined ASM in 1946, becoming Chief Development Engineer (Propeller Turbines). In 1949-50 he was attached to the British Joint Services Mission in the USA at the NACA Lewis Laboratory. He became Quality Control Manager in 1958, supervising all aspects of quality for aero engines, diesel engines and cars. When the Power Division came along he retained his leadership of the Quality Control function and subsequently in IMD.

A graduate of London University, the author was involved in combustion research and development, firstly with de Havilland Engines and from 1947 with Armstrong Siddeley. Following the creation of the Power Division he was seconded to Maybach in Friedrichshafen for a couple of years. On returning to Ansty he was involved in projects, notably the RB223 and Industrial Olympus 593. Latterly he was Product Manager Marine Spey.

The grass roots

It is quite impossible in this account to recall more than just a few of the more prominent names in the history of Ansty. Somewhat arbitrarily some of those surviving from the early days, together with the more obvious persons from the top have been included. But this excludes those heroes remaining unsung who added the vital ingredient in translating policies into practice either by mind or by hand. Theirs was sometimes the greater contribution. Their input was crucial as was their enthusiasm for the job.

Industrial disputes on the site were rare, due in no small part to the goodwill of enlightened attitudes in both directions. By and large, Ansty was a happy ship, the feeling of wellbeing being enhanced by the success of the mainline products.

EPILOGUE

The story of events on the site since work began in 1935 provides a prime example of the way in which a modern industrial enterprise had to adapt to changing circumstances. Connected with the aviation industry the business followed the drastic transformations of its parents both in war and peace. The need for change was always present.

The managements of the immediate post war era had very difficult choices to make. Traditionally the business had been mostly that of supply of equipment for national defence and therefore subject to contract with the government. The rapid developments in defence technology after the Second World War had meant that the business was unstable and it became clear that dependence on such work, widely regarded as secure, albeit at relatively low profit, was indeed a high risk business. Following the cancellation of the contract for the engines of the Avro supersonic bomber, H T Chapman, Managing Director of Armstrong Siddeley declared that the Company had put too much emphasis on government work and on aero engines in particular. Overnight ASM's turnover had been reduced by a third with little prospect of filling the gap for some considerable time. The consequence was the shotgun marriage with Bristol. A considerable programme of diversification starting with ASM and continuing in the Power Division of Bristol Siddeley had led to products well suited to manufacture by the precision and quality methods of the aero engine industry. But within a couple of decades all of these, excepting the main line activities of marine and industrial gas turbines and some residual work on underwater weapons, had disappeared. Indeed, of the dozen major enterprises on the site since 1935 only two survived for more than a brief spell. It became clearer that there was no golden road to survival. The imperative of finding out what the world wanted and making it at the right price had been well understood by John Siddeley and was well understood by his successors. It seemed that a mixture of government and commercial business would be the way forward.

In the years of rapid expansion in the 1970s such a mix of business was achieved and it was outstandingly successful, creating an enterprise of significance on a world scale. Even so, as this decade went on the threat of uncontrolled rise in cost of the hardware emerged. As a predominately design and marketing organisation, and dependent for a large proportion of its supply on the Aero Division, Ansty had less control over its costs than it might otherwise have had. Increases in the cost of manufacture from both the Aero Divisions and from elsewhere seriously eroded profit margins and by 1982 when this chronicle ends, drastic change was once more called for.

The Historical Series is published as a joint initiative by the Rolls-Royce Heritage Trust and The Sir Henry Royce Memorial Foundation.

Also published in the series:
- No.1 Rolls-Royce – the formative years 1906-1939
  Alec Harvey-Bailey RRHT 2nd edition 1983 (out of print)
- No.2 The Merlin in perspective – the combat years
  Alec Harvey-Bailey, RRHT 4th edition 1995
- No.3 Rolls-Royce – the pursuit of excellence
  Alec Harvey-Bailey and Mike Evans, HRMF 1984
- No.4 In the beginning – the Manchester origins of Rolls-Royce
  Mike Evans, RRHT 1984
- No.5 Rolls-Royce – the Derby Bentleys
  Alec Harvey-Bailey, HRMF 1985
- No.6 The early days of Rolls-Royce – and the Montagu family
  Lord Montagu of Beaulieu, RRHT 1986
- No.7 Rolls-Royce – Hives, the quiet tiger
  Alec Harvey-Bailey, HRMF 1985
- No.8 Rolls-Royce – Twenty to Wraith
  Alec Harvey-Bailey, HRMF 1986
- No.9 Rolls-Royce and the Mustang
  David Birch, RRHT 1987
- No.10 From Gipsy to Gem with diversions, 1926-1986
  Peter Stokes, RRHT 1987
- No.11 Armstrong Siddeley – the Parkside story, 1896-1939
  Ray Cook, RRHT 1989
- No.12 Henry Royce – mechanic
  Donald Bastow, RRHT 1989
- No.14 Rolls-Royce – the sons of Martha
  Alec Harvey-Bailey, HRMF 1989
- No.15 Olympus – the first forty years
  Alan Baxter, RRHT 1990
- No.16 Rolls-Royce piston aero engines – a designer remembers
  A A Rubbra, RRHT 1990
- No.17 Charlie Rolls – pioneer aviator
  Gordon Bruce, RRHT 1990
- No.18 The Rolls-Royce Dart – pioneering turboprop
  Roy Heathcote, RRHT 1992
- No.19 The Merlin 100 series – the ultimate military development
  Alec Harvey-Bailey and Dave Piggott, RRHT 1993
- No.20 Rolls-Royce – Hives' turbulent barons
  Alec Harvey-Bailey, HRMF 1992
- No.21 Rolls-Royce – The Crecy Engine
  Nahum, Foster-Pegg, Birch, RRHT 1994
- No.22 Vikings at Waterloo – the wartime work on the Whittle jet engine by the Rover Company
  David S Brooks, RRHT 1997
- No.23 Rolls-Royce – the first cars from Crewe
  Ken Lea, RRHT 1997
- No.24 The Rolls-Royce Tyne
  Lionel Haworth, RRHT 1998

Special Sectioned Drawings of piston aero engines
      L Jones, 1995

Technical Series:
- No.1   Rolls-Royce and the Rateau Patents
  H Pearson, RRHT 1989
- No.2   The vital spark! The development of aero engine sparking plugs
  K Gough, RRHT 1991
- No.3   The performance of a supercharged aero engine
  S Hooker, H Reed and A Yarker, RRHT 1997

Books are available from:
Rolls-Royce Heritage Trust, Rolls-Royce plc, Moor Lane, PO Box 31, Derby DE24 8BJ